I LOVE
SHELTIES
ANNUAL 2022

Tecassia
PUBLISHING

Published in 2021 by

Tecassia
PUBLISHING

Tecassia Publishing
Building 31186
PO Box 6945
London
W1A 6US
www.tecassia.com

ISBN

Hardback 978-1-913916-09-1
Paperback 978-1-913916-10-7

Also available as an e-book 978-1-913916-08-4

Designed by Camilla Fellas Arnold

Dedication

✿ ✿

Dedicated to Angel, Ash, Robbie and Flash that were all featured in last year's annual but have since gone to rainbow bridge.

Run free, dear shelties, until we meet again!

✿ ✿

A portion of the proceeds of this book will be donated to
Yorkshire Shetland Sheepdog Club Rescue
www.yssc.co.uk

Hello & Welcome

🐾 🐾 🐾 🐾 🐾 🐾 🐾 🐾 🐾 🐾 🐾 🐾 🐾 🐾 🐾 🐾 🐾 🐾 🐾
🐾 🐾 🐾 🐾 🐾 🐾 🐾 🐾 🐾 🐾 🐾 🐾 🐾 🐾 🐾 🐾 🐾 🐾 🐾

I've dreamt of creating sheltie books for so long and had the idea for a sheltie annual quite a few years ago. I kept putting it off for a multitude of reasons but when the idea resurfaced in summer 2020 I decided to go for it and quickly put a call out for submissions.

I was bowled away by how the sheltie community came together and got involved in the first edition. In the *I Love Shelties Annual 2021* we featured over 150 different shelties from all over the world!

Sales from the first edition raised £300 (approx $415 USD) for the English Shetland Sheepdog Club's Welfare and Rescue Co-ordination Division and I can't wait to see how much we can raise for *Yorkshire Shetland Sheepdog Club Rescue* this year.

It's been amazing to see both new and familiar faces from last year's annual sending in more photos for this year. It is my hope that we can continue creating this annual for many year's to come. So most of all, thank YOU for your support, whether you sent us photos and stories or bought a copy (or copies!) We honestly couldn't make this annual without you.

Forever grateful,

Camilla

Camilla Fellas Arnold

Editor in Chief

CONTENTS

MEET OUR COVER STAR!

Meet Aline (Pedigree name Diamond Rain Flower Aline), born in Szolnok (Hungary) in 2013. She came to our family as a simple family dog but even then we saw that she was more than simply a dog.

🐾 🐾 🐾 🐾 🐾 🐾 🐾 🐾 🐾 🐾 🐾 🐾 🐾
🐾 🐾 🐾 🐾 🐾 🐾 🐾 🐾 🐾 🐾 🐾 🐾 🐾
🐾 🐾 🐾 🐾 🐾 🐾 🐾 🐾 🐾 🐾 🐾 🐾 🐾

We've learned a lot of tricks together and she has been doing agility with me. In 2017, everything changed when we entered our first show. We thought we would try this too because a lot of people commented on Aline's beauty. So although I didn't like the shows, I thought it was worth a try.

However, I decided if Aline didn't enjoy going, I wouldn't force it. But she surprised me as she really enjoyed it and knew from the first minute what she had to do. I was very proud of her.

From then on there was no stopping. So far we have participated in 21 exhibitions and we hope we will still take part in many more events. Aline is a multiple champion and holds many show titles. At the end of 2021, we will be taking part in the biggest competition to be held in Hungary at the European dog show.

But it's not just exhibitions that exist in our lives. We love to hike and enjoy every minute spent together. I really like photographing Aline so it's a special privilege to have my photo on the cover of this fantastic book.

Pixel, 2 and Reglisse, 1 in the Bondy Forest, France

A LEGION OF FANS

We're so honoured by all the positive feedback we received about last year's annual. We have 40 reviews on Amazon which is incredible! We also had lots of people send in their photos of their pups enjoying the annual, some are even reading their own stories!

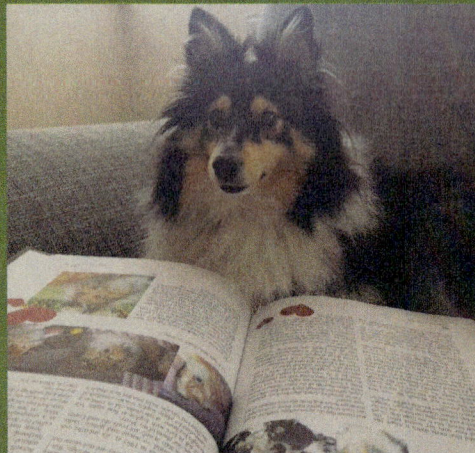

Left top to bottom: Joy, Dory, Wee Charlie and Teddy. Right top to bottom: Tally and Tina, Charlie and Gracie and Mom

Special Surprise

In the first annual I told the story of how my family got started with shetland sheepdogs and it was all down to my grandad's suggestion. He had no idea I'd be sharing our story, nor that I was dedicating the first annual to him – he was so excited when he found out! I simply had to get a picture of him, our current pack and the annual.

MILLIE THE MAGNIFICENT

AND HER DEATH DEFYING TALE

I still remember the exact moment Millie made her entrance into the world. It was at home on 3rd May 2013. When you see a puppy born right in front of your eyes you can't help but fall in love instantly. We were meant to be together.

Millie has suffered from a sensitive tummy from a puppy. In the summer of 2020, Millie was diagnosed with Campylobacter – an infectious bacterial disease, usually self-limiting. Then, at one of her vet check-ups in September, it was identified that Millie had a low-grade heart murmur. Millie was booked in for a heart scan in mid-October.

In the early hours of 8th October, Millie was violently sick. At the vets, she was given pain relief and the standard anti-sickness injection. We came home but Millie was sick again

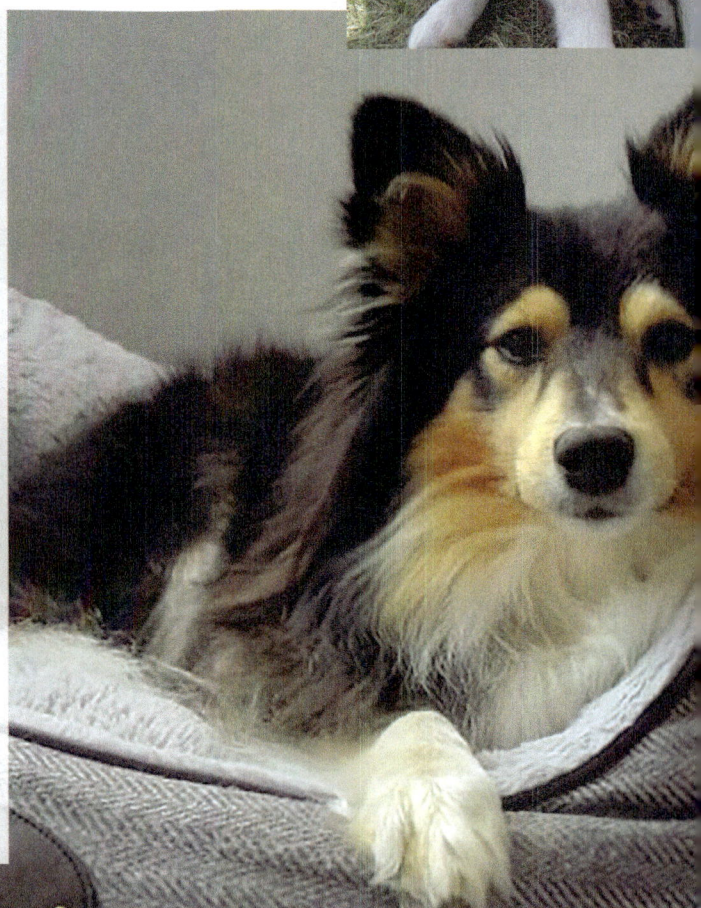

twice. Back at the vets, I knew something serious was going on. As the vet came out to collect her, Millie went flat in the back of the car. She struggled to get up and walk. I carried her to the door of the vets and left her there that night.

The following morning the vets called. They had carried out the heart scan, x-rays and ultrasounds. They found her stomach dilated and her intestines were barely moving. They suspected a blockage possibly from a foreign body.

Surgery was performed. The vet found and removed a tampon she had ingested. I was horrified! The vet didn't know how long it had been there; it caused severe intestinal inflammation because of toxic build up. The vets wanted to remove the inflamed and damaged parts of the intestines, however, there was too much to remove to allow Millie a good quality of life. Millie's only option was to hope and pray that the body healed itself. She stayed on IV fluids, antibiotics, and gut motility medication for two nights. But when Millie refused to eat

and drink at the vets they sent her home.

The next day there was no improvement. Back at the vets again, I could see the vet's concern about her lack of progress. There were now two options. 1: Try a further course of IV fluids and medications. 2: Put Millie to sleep. I was preparing myself for a very difficult decision, but I wasn't ready to give up just yet. I have never been more scared in my life.

Another two nights at the vets and a lot of prayers worked a miracle; Millie made slow progress much to everyone's delight. Our vets and vet nurses hold a soft spot for Millie.

Millie made a full recovery and is now back to her loveable self – albeit with a big dietary and lifestyle change. We have all adapted well and she enjoys a quiet life.

I absolutely love dogs, I can't ask for anything else right now.

Take care fellow Sheltonians!

Jenny Austin, Reading, England

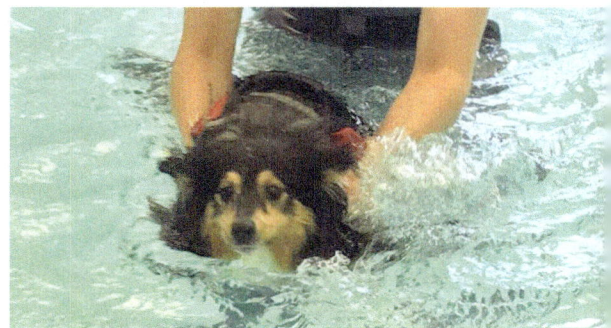

FENTON GOES FORTH

OUR YEAR CAPTURING THE 2022 CALENDAR

It's safe to say that 2021 has been an eventful time for us here in Shetland. I can honestly say it has been one of the worst years I have ever known weather-wise.

We started the year with violent winds driving some pretty bitter blizzards across the land – getting to work certainly proved very interesting at times as the roads pretty much disappeared! The snow eventually melted but the sharp north winds remained, continuing right to the end of spring and causing some difficult times for both farmers and their livestock as crops refused to grow.

The sun very rarely made an appearance even through summer and before you knew it, winter was starting to creep in again with the long, dark nights making an appearance once more. As you can imagine, this has made creating our photos a rather... challenging experience!

Photographs and story by Kaylee Garrick

Fearing I wouldn't get enough for a calendar, I decided that the gang and I would take some shots inside. Some of these turned out lovely, particularly the sunflower and Christmas ones. However, they caused some hilarity between the neighbours as I take these photos in my kitchen standing on top of a table, usually in my pyjamas... maybe I should have closed the curtains? The look on the delivery man's face was certainly a picture when I caught his eye whilst halfway through a shoot!

I get the feeling the people of Shetland are just used to my antics now and don't ask any more questions these days. We've certainly had fun creating the 2022 calendar that's for sure and here are some more stories behind the photos.

✤ ✤
✤ ✤
✤ ✤

"The Mermaid Shot" – Meal Beach (Burra Isle)

The mermaid one is what is known as a "cursed shot", meaning that everything that could have gone wrong while trying to take it, did. For those of you who own the 2021 calendar, the pirate photo was the same and took four attempts to get. The first attempt for this photo was during a beautiful crisp February day.

The location was Meal beach in Burra – quite a common spot for us to appear and take photos as it's quite close to our house and the place is stunning. I had taken the dogs down for a runaround and play before grabbing a quick snap of them with their little boats.

When I got back and uploaded the photos they were just a bit bland. I didn't like the composition and decided to just redo the whole thing. What could possibly go wrong?

Attempt number two, me and my mam, aka my camera assistant hiked down to the beach (again) with all the kit, props and of course the supermodels to be met with PERFECT conditions on glistening white sands. It could not have been better. The light was in the right position, the tide was out revealing a nice little spot where the dogs got lined up. I aimed the camera, aaaaand... DEAD! My battery had decided to give up and there wasn't enough juice to get even one photo. I was gutted!

Attempt number three; I woke up to the sun shining and thought, "fantastic, this is it! This is the day I will finally get that mermaid photo!". Another drive to the beach and hike down onto the sand. It was looking good. My battery was charged (I now have a spare after the last incident.) The dogs got into position, I aimed and then DARKNESS! Where did the sun go? I looked up bewildered to find that out of nowhere a great big, black and rather stormy looking cloud had formed, completely blocking the sun and what little light we had.

Needless to say, a few choice words were said towards the sky gods who were no doubt having a right good laugh at my suffering. I gathered up my kit again and hiked up the hill. But that wasn't the end of that session. No, the trickster god Loki had another little prank up his sleeve at the expense of this poor little exhausted photographer.

After I had counted (and double-counted) the pups in the back of the car then checked to ensure my camera kit was there, I began to head for home slowly backing myself out of the parking space until I heard a rather loud, soul sinking CRACK. Immediately, I knew what it was. I had forgotten to put the boat props back into the car. The destruction that met my eyes when I got out of the car was heart-wrenching.

I had spent hours modifying these little ships ready to be used as props and there was all my effort spread across the ground in bits. I could have laid there and cried but what was that going to achieve? So I picked up the pieces,

headed for home and warmed up the glue gun. We finally got the shot on attempt number four and I was so relieved and happy to finally see all that work come together in my mermaid creation. But know when you turn your calendar over and look at that shot, there's more of a tale to those large fishy tails than meets the eye!

Prop and equipment failures are not uncommon for us like what happened here. For the police photo, my flash decided it wouldn't work and I've lost count of how many times a peaky blinders flat cap flew off! However, you just have to remain patient, carry on and well... laugh!

" Vikings" – The Skidbladner (Unst)

One of my all-time favourite shots is the Viking photo. There was quite a lot of work that went into the costumes for this one but they turned out great.

There could only be one location for this photo and that had to be next to the Skidbladner, a full-sized replica Viking ship which was built by a Swedish crew attempting to replicate the journey taken by Lief Erikson from Scandinavia to America.

The ship, unfortunately, ran into problems around the harsh seas surrounding Shetland but thankfully all on board were okay. However, the mission was aborted and the ship never made it across the pond.

She now sits proudly next to a Viking longhouse in Unst, the most northerly island in the UK. It's a fantastic place to visit, particularly if you have a passion for Viking heritage, but getting there can certainly be an experience. It takes a couple of hours driving from Scalloway where I'm from and includes two ferry journeys; one to get onto the island of Yell and then another to Unst.

We, mam and I, breathed a sigh of relief when we finally set foot on location as we had only taken a small amount of cash with us that day and found that the card machine on the ferries had broken. We had JUST enough to get us across. We then discovered that there were no shops and my car was running low on fuel but thankfully we found a small place on Unst.

We'd taken a bit of time to get set up but I was finally ready to grab my shot when suddenly I heard my mam gasp and go "omg!" behind me. I turned around to find a political convoy had appeared. A young local SNP candidate stepped out from his logo adorned car and was delighted to find he'd caught the "famous dogs" in action!

He very politely asked if he could grab a photo with them, to which I replied "well, you'd better take a prop with you then!"

laughing as I handed him a small axe that had been in Fenton's mouth.

It was a brilliant photo and shared far and wide across social media. It took a couple of attempts at different angles and lighting to get the perfect Viking shot after this, but it turned out fantastic in the end.

We're often surrounded by loving onlookers at our photoshoots. What can I say, the gang are A-list celebs after all!

Recently, we almost caused a crash in the middle of town while we were trying to capture a photo at a lighthouse sculpture. Also, we were once met by someone from Australia who had recognised us while we were out in the middle of nowhere on a walk. She came running over the hill saying, "I can't believe it! The famous dogs!" It was so funny!

Each dog has their own mini fan base with Thiago's being the strongest for sure!

Honestly, the funniest photo I have ever taken and the closest I have ever come to dying with laughter was trying to get this shot. I had the idea of dressing them up as bikers for ages and finally set about finding costumes for it this year. I come from a family of bikers myself and enjoy long but rather cold journeys on my Suzuki "Intruder" cruiser during my days off.

"Biker photo" – WWII base (Lerwick)

The final touch to their outfits was the beards which I thought would look great, but I never quite realised how utterly hilarious and ridiculous they would be on the gang. I tried the first one on Gimli and two minutes later found myself on the ground gasping for air and completely helpless. The "moustache" part of the beard pushed up her top lip, making her look as though she was giving me a cheeky grin. I found this happened to every dog I put it on and it just looked so so funny.

I eventually managed to locate a small motorbike prop from a friend of mine and then we were off on location to finally grab the shot. I'd chosen one of the old bunkers up at the WWII base in Lerwick as it seemed to give the dark and mysterious vibe I was after.

I had spied the place while we were taking the Batman photos and thought it would be perfect. It's quite a hike to get to, particularly with the amount of stuff we had to drag there, so we ended up having to stop and rest a couple of times.

We were also in a slight panic to get the photo done before the mist rolled in from the sea as we could see it approaching on the horizon slowly but surely. The location has a really interesting history and believe it or not, Shetland had more of an involvement in the war than what you would suspect. The islands were well sought after by Nazi Germany as we would have provided the perfect stepping stone onto Orkney and then Scotland.

After Norway was taken over, the government placed 20,000 soldiers in Shetland, essentially doubling our population, and garrisoned them at various points around the islands to protect them. The first bomb to touch British soil was in Shetland, up north at Sullom. Thankfully they missed their target completely and the only fatality was

a poor bunny, giving rise to the song "Run Rabbit Run" which then became very popular during that era.

Many locals also assisted in the "Shetland Bus" rescue which included small fishing boats sneaking in and out of Norway to transport people out and supplies in to support the Norwegians in crises. The location we were heading for in Lerwick used to have large guns pointing out from it which saw action several times and shot down quite a few planes in their time. Sadly, they're no longer there for people to see.

We managed to get there just in time and get the supermodels ready but I struggled to get the shot for laughing so much. I grabbed the photo JUST in time before the mist suddenly plunged us into darkness and I'm happy to say, it turned out great!
This was a remake we decided to do of a photo I took a couple of years ago. The original was done on a set of steps in Scalloway and caused a lot of hilarity with the locals walking past. I loved it, but I believed I could do it better.

I'd seen the perfect location for the shot online as well at Brough Lodge on

"Ghost Busters" – Brough Lodge (Fetlar)

the island of Fetlar up north. This is a remarkable location with a history dating back to the early 1800s. The original owner of the site, however, was a bit of a tyrant and responsible for much of the "Shetland clearances" when people were forced out of their houses in favour of sheep.

Sadly, much of the location has fallen into significant disrepair and we had to have special permission to enter the site and take photos. I would love to see the buildings restored and the history of the place kept alive as it is very important to the islands. Getting there is certainly a challenge. Even more so than getting to Unst.

Our first attempt failed as we drove up to the pier, only to realise that there are a VERY limited number of ferries that travel to Fetlar at the weekend and we had missed the only one in the morning.

For our second attempt, I decided to be a bit more organised and book ourselves on the ferries getting there, something that should be reasonably simple, but somehow we ended up going from Toft to Yell, to Unst, BACK to Yell and THEN finally to Fetlar! It was quite the trip taking four ferries and several hours to get there. The weather wasn't in our favour either so getting the photos was

We were advised to go to the ferry at its departure time to see if they could "squeeze" us on, but otherwise, we'd be stuck on this tiny island in the middle of nowhere until the next day. Thankfully, there is a small cafe/shop so we headed for there to stock up on supplies in case we found ourselves camping for the night. The lady working there was just as shocked as we were saying she'd never seen so many folks on the island and commented there were sheepdog trials ongoing as well as folk from the RSPB investigating the birds there.

At the time of ferry departure, we sat very nervously and watched as the cars began to queue up at the terminal and sure enough, it was going to be a very full boat. But, somehow by an absolute miracle, the crew managed to get us on the ferry. I have never felt so relieved. It was a tight squeeze for sure, but we were finally heading for home.

Capturing the photos for our calendar is always a challenge. Shetland weather is always pretty wild and very unpredictable; the locations we take each shot are usually in the middle of nowhere and require several hours and ferries to get to; the kit and props are very heavy and awkward to carry over often coarse terrain; and of course, the models take a lot of work to train and groom too. There are days where the gang just go, "you know what... I'm not feeling this today", which means we have to stop and go for the photo another time.

difficult but we managed. Thankfully, it was the "Halloween" style shot so it's meant to look dark and spooky!

It then came time to try and get home again so I went online to try and book ourselves back, only to discover that there was no ferry back. I managed to get a hold of the operator who told me that the only ferry in the afternoon was fully booked which is something that NEVER happens. But for some reason on that particular day, (of course, it would have to be the one day we also decided to travel!), there were no spaces.

The best piece of photography advice I can give you is that sad dogs don't take nice photos! Keep them happy and make it a game. It has been a pleasure to tell you all about what goes on in the background of these shots.

I cannot wait to see what 2022 brings and we already have loads of ideas for new photos! We will hopefully be launching our "FenWalks Challenge" in the middle of it all too so keep your eyes on this space, we're going on an adventure!

HALL OF FAME

We received so many photos and stories in the making of this book from shelties and their owners all around the world. We wanted to include as many beautiful faces as possible so welcome to our sheltie 'hall of fame'! Can you spot any shelties you know?

Indiana Bones, 'Indy' at 10 weeks from the UK

Leone, 2 from Ottawa, Ontario, Canada

Pepper, 6 from Milnrow, Rochdale, UK

Sundanze, 6 from Melbourne Australia

Chip and Fizz (mother and son) from the UK

Bernie and Rolo from Torquay UK

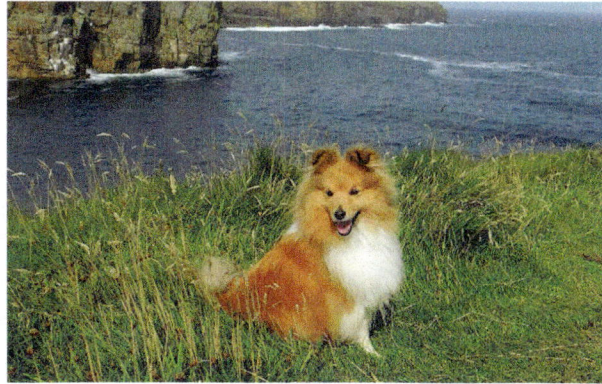

Wee Charlie, 10 from Scotland

Chico, 6 and his inseparable pal Obi (born in March 2021) from the UK

Pandora, blue merle age 6 and Dice, tricolour, age 8 from Newmarket, Suffolk, UK

Sasha, 11 and Maisie,
1 from the New Forest,
Ringwood UK

Gracie celebrating her 9th birthday in
Raleigh, North Carolina, USA and Badger at
8 weeks old from Cambridgeshire, UK

Dex, 12 from California, USA

Shadow, 7.5 and Onyx, 5 from Brisbane
Australia

L to R: Rosco, 4, Dylan, 7 months and
Harley, 8 Sunderland UK

Echo, Encore, and Picardy in Centerville,
Ohio, USA

Harris 5, Copper 18 months and Tummel 7, on the Isle of Harris

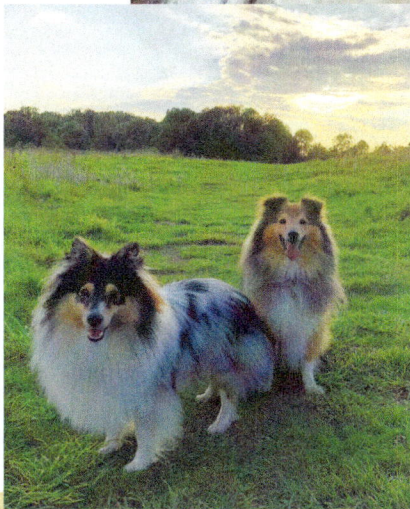

Malchy, 6 and Frosty, 1 from East Anglia, UK

Laddie, 8 from Hull in East Yorkshire UK

Roxy, 6 from Hayling Island, UK

L to R: Perry, 9 and Harvey, 5 in Shetland at Sumburgh Lighthouse

Lucky Star, 4 from Middletown, Delaware, USA

Saphie and Elsa in Norfolk UK

Pepsi, 9 from Scalloway Shetland

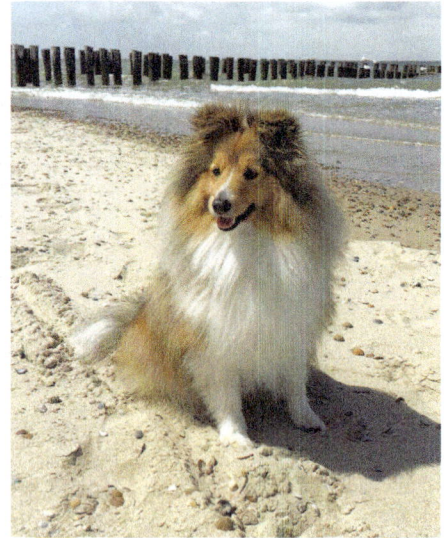

Tommie, 5 on the beach at Domburg, The Netherlands

Smudge, 1.5 and Kyle, 13 weeks old from Ipswich, Suffolk, UK

L to R: Aisee, Kassi, Kermes, Sesse, Silver and Amigo aged 4-12 years old at Damsbo forest, Denmark

Sonny and Teddy in the UK

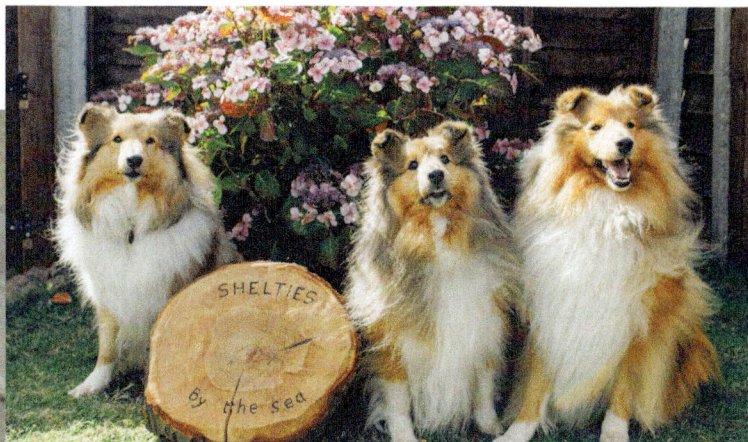

L to R: Talia, 2, Mia, 6 and Teddy, 3 from Norfolk UK

Chip, 2 from Fort Worth, Texas, USA

Cali, 3 from Berkshire, UK

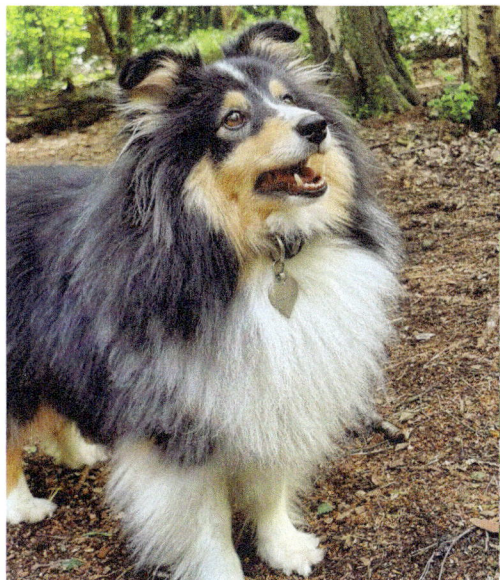

Keeko, 6 from Arbroath, Angus Scotland among the crocuses with pal Charlie

Meka, Zoe, Jordie, Charli, Bryn,Fergus and Cricket from New Zealand

Lexi, 1 from Bristol, UK

MacAllan and Ziggy, affectionately known as Mac & Cheese in the UK

Poppy, 6 months enjoying the delights of Epping Forest, UK

L to R: Skye, Trudi, Teazle, Heidi, Dandy, Jamie from the UK

Athena, 2 from Queensland, Australia

L to R: Nessie, 2, Bentley, 9 months old, Milly, 8.5 and Lincoln 4 from Queensland, Australia

Onyx, Drifter and Skye at Castlerigg Stone Circle, Lake District, UK

Mila Flo and Pearl photographed by Abigail Harris

SASHI'S STORY BECAME A BOOK!

✿ ✿ ✿ ✿ ✿ ✿ ✿ ✿ ✿ ✿ ✿ ✿ ✿ ✿
✿ ✿ ✿ ✿ ✿ ✿ ✿ ✿ ✿ ✿ ✿ ✿ ✿ ✿
✿ ✿ ✿ ✿ ✿ ✿ ✿ ✿ ✿ ✿ ✿ ✿ ✿ ✿

I adopted Sashi in December 2001 from Shetland Sheepdog Placement Services of New Jersey (Aneita Frey). She had been turned over to an all-breed shelter because her original family couldn't deal with her "excessive herding instinct". Thankfully, SSPSNJ took Sashi from the shelter and kept her safe while interviewing applicants for her "forever home".

Shelties were bred in the Shetland Islands to herd sheep. They make a wonderful companion dog – funny, loving, full of zest and extremely intelligent! They love to please their owners and are easily trained in obedience, herding, agility and nose work.

Because of their breeding, they are very vocal (barky) and are hard-wired to chase anything that moves (running children, joggers, bikes, of course sheep and unfortunately, cars). Obedience training can help them control these urges when directed at less desirable objects.

In Sashi's case, her first two and a half

Sashi The Scared Little Sheltie, *Sashi Adopts a Brother* and *Sashi and The Puppy Mill Girl* are available to purchase on Amazon

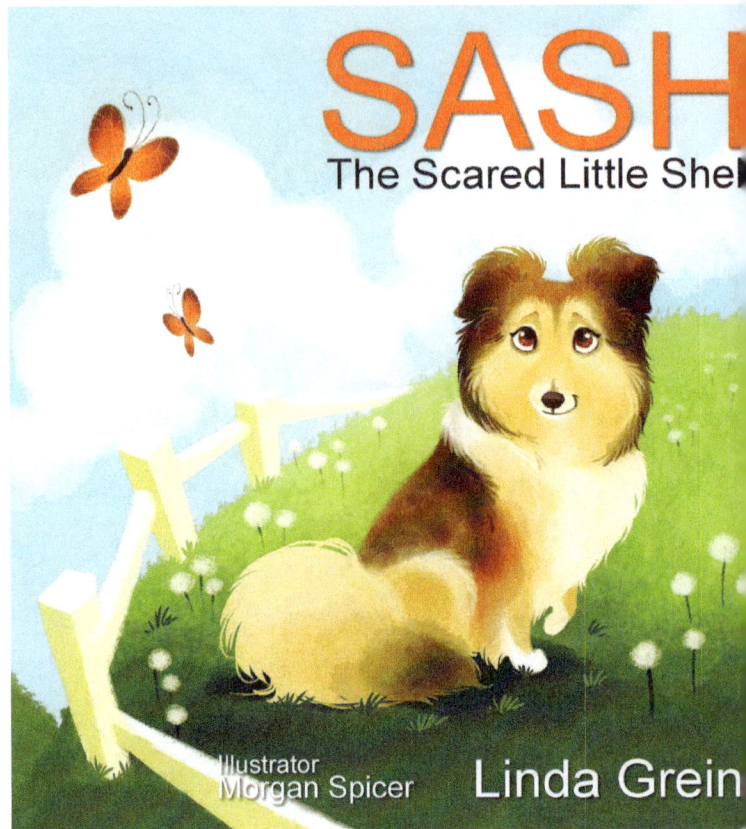

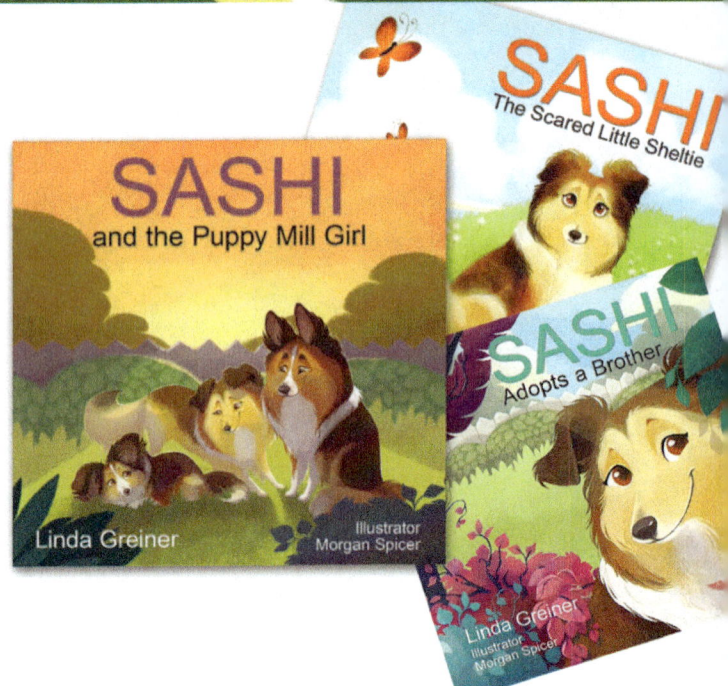

> **I soon realised that she didn't know how to play or go up/down stairs... Anything she considered new or strange in the house would send her running to the safety of whatever she could hide behind.**

years of life weren't happy. She had never been socialised as a puppy or exposed to much of anything that could be considered positive. She came home with me as a terrified bundle of fur and wouldn't let me near her for petting or cuddling.

I soon realised that she didn't know how to play or go up/down stairs, was terrified of trashcans and other objects on the sidewalk, even decorative flags flapping in the wind would cause her to bark and cringe.

Anything she considered new or strange in the house would send her running to the safety of whatever she could hide behind. It was very stressful to walk her because she'd lunge and bark at people, animals and cars. She was extremely afraid of being petted by anyone she didn't know well, backing away from the 'open palm' even when approached slowly, down on her level and with a treat. This is the result of being hit during her 'previous life'.

Time, patience, training and most of all love helped her conquer a number of these problems. We did several classes at Wonderdogs in Marlton NJ and Allens Kennels in Moorestown NJ.

🐾 🐾 🐾 🐾 🐾 🐾 🐾 🐾 🐾 🐾 🐾 🐾 🐾

Sashi came a long way in her first 18 months, learning to trust and gaining the self confidence to try new things. It can take more than two years to rehabilitate a rescue dog, depending on the degree of physical and/or emotional trauma they've gone through and my little angel had more than her share which you can read about in Sashi The Scared Little Sheltie with the follow-ups Sashi Adopts a Brother and Sashi and The Puppy Mill Girl.

All three books were written with the intention of educating parents of young children about the Shetland Sheepdog and how love and patience is used to transform your dog into the happy and well-adjusted pet they are meant to be.

Linda Greiner

PUPPY FEVER

Shelties are gorgeous at any age but there's something extra special about those little tiny bundles of fluff that melts every heart. Highly recommend any time you need a pick me up, just open this page, but be warned – you will be broody for another puppy if you do!

A basket of puppies, what more could one want? How about four puppies sleeping in a row! Meet Bowie, Freddie, Pundit and Rio.

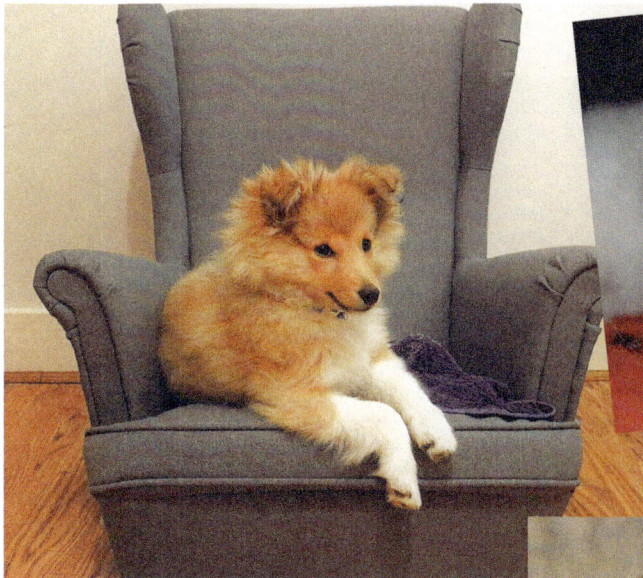

Little Ernesto sitting pretty in his own chair

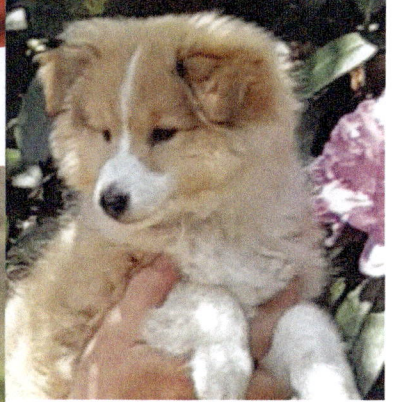

Pretty sure there's a puppy called Bentley hidden underneath all that fluff!

Talia sitting pretty in the flowers

Frosty and Malchy fell in love at first sight when they met. There's nothing better than puppy kisses!

GONE BUT NOT FORGOTTEN

"

It is because of Sammy, I fell in love with shelties and went on to own my four beautiful girls that are with me still.

The first time I saw Sammy, he was in a small wire cage on the floor in a back room of a pet shop in Malacca, Malaysia. The room was full of cages containing different breeds of dogs. The Chinese lady opened the door and reached in to grab Sammy and pull him out. He was afraid of her and cowered down and he ran over to me and crouched by my feet as soon as she let go. I scooped him up in my arms and took him out to my car.

The lady followed me asking 'did I want the cage as well?' I told her that he would never go in a cage again. I drove the hour and a half journey home, lifted Sammy out of the car, and let him explore his new home and garden. For the first few nights he would sleep out by the patio, then gradually he became less fearful and came closer. Finally, I encouraged him onto the sofa for cuddles.

He was such a lovely boy, so very gentle and loving. He was terrified of men and would run and hide whenever my friend Harry came over. I took Sammy down to the local beach and he saw the sea for the first time in his life. I was told that he was six years old but the vet said he was much older, more like ten or eleven.

Sadly, we were not together very long. One night while he was out on the patio, he came in contact with a poisonous frog. I didn't know that at the time. I simply wondered why he was taking so long outside. He came indoors, licking his lips. I thought he wanted a drink.

We went to bed but he woke me up in the night very sick. There were no emergency vets available so as soon as the vet opened I phoned them. Harry and I put Sammy in the car. Harry drove while I sat in the back holding Sammy in my arms. When we got to vet and carried him in the vet said at once he had been poisoned.

We left Sammy there on a drip while the vet tried to save his life, but later that afternoon I received the dreaded phone call that he had passed away. Later that day, I found the frog round the back of the shed. The vet confirmed that was the cause of Sammy's death.

Sammys time with me was very short but I know that he enjoyed those last weeks of his life. He had freedom from life in a cage.

It is because of Sammy, I fell in love with shelties and went on to own my four beautiful girls that are with me still. Sammy will never be forgotten.

Sammy came to me on 29th December 2011 and he left me on 17th February 2012.

Lisa's love of shelties continues in her story of *The Maylasian Sheltie Girls* on page 40.

Photographs and story by Lisa Brown

Photographs and story by Lisa Brown

THE MALAYSIAN SHELTIE GIRLS

How four very special shelties moved across the world from Malaysia to enjoy spring blossoms and winter snow in the United Kingdom

"I knew the girls would have to endure a very long flight and I wanted to get them prepared well in advance so I started the process ten months before we were due to leave.

🐾 🐾
🐾 🐾
🐾 🐾

In 2012 I was living in Port Dickson, Malaysia, when four very special shelties entered my life. They were: Enya, Glory, Gracie and Blossom.

Enya and Glory were born on the 3rd of February, 2012 to their mum Blossom, who was six years old at the time. Following the sudden and tragic death of my previous sheltie Sammy, I had been looking on the internet and found a sheltie breeder on the outskirts of Kuala Lumpur.

I contacted her and she invited me to go and visit. She told me her dog Blossom had recently given birth to 5 puppies – all girls. She had another dog Aimee who was due to give birth any time.

On the 22nd of February, I went to visit Blossom's puppies. When I arrived they were all asleep in a basket, five cute little bundles of fluff.

As I knelt on the floor to have a closer look one of them woke up. She clambered over her sleeping sisters to lick my hand and touch me with her tiny paw. I picked her up and held her, enchanted by the pretty white blaze and knew she was mine. Her name was going to be Enya. On that very same night, Aimee gave birth to her puppies; three boys and three girls. When I looked at them, one in particular, caught my eye, a tri-colour girl with a huge white collar. She would later become my Gracie only I didn't know it at the time.

L–R: Glory, Gracie and Enya. Inset: Mum Blossom

When it became time to collect Enya and bring her home I decided that she would need a playmate. I was won over by her sister Glory and so brought two puppies home. The breeder then asked me if I also wanted to give a home to their mum Blossom, as she was being retired from breeding.

At first, I wasn't sure how it would work out but then agreed, and so my sheltie family became a trio.

A few months later and I learnt from the breeder that all the puppies had gone to new homes except for one – Gracie. Originally someone did want her but then changed their mind with the insane excuse that 'she was not pretty enough'! I didn't hesitate. I told the breeder to bring Gracie to me. Our family became four and we were now complete.

We noticed after a while that Gracie had a problem with one of her back legs, and so we introduced her to the swimming pool. She loved it and became so confident she would just leap in from the side. Over time all the girls, even Blossom, went in the pool every day. It was great exercise for them, and they really enjoyed themselves. My friend Harry, would take them swimming every morning for an hour or more.

He enjoyed it as much as they did. The girls' days were filled with swimming, walks to the beach and playtimes in the garden and around the house. We had to be careful of dangerous creatures though, such as snakes, centipedes, large lizards and sea eagles that hovered over the garden. Eventually, the time came when we had to leave Malaysia. To say goodbye to our old way of life and begin a new life in England. I knew the girls would have to endure a very long flight and I wanted to get them prepared well in advance, so I started the process ten months before we were due to leave.

We had to buy four special airline approved flight crates. These took a while to order, as they had to be imported from, of all places; England!

When they arrived, my friend Harry and I assembled them without the doors. We

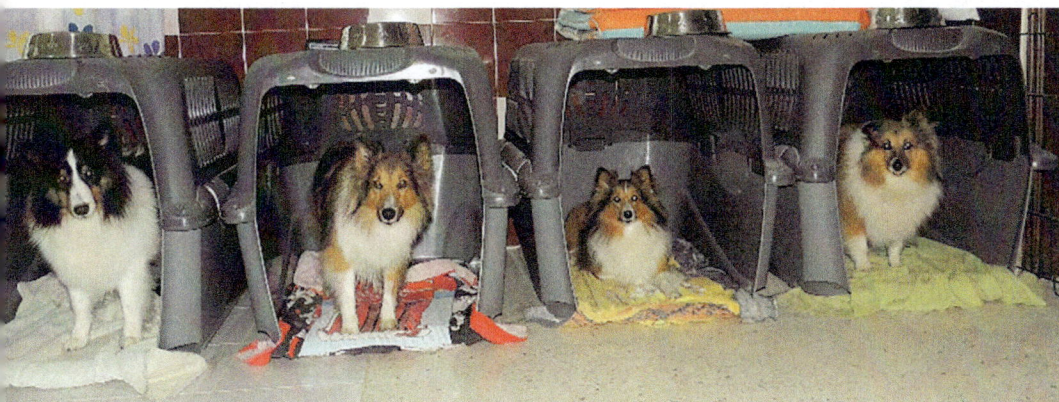

Crate Training Preparation For The Girls To Travel From Malaysia To The UK

set them up in my bedroom so the girls could investigate and get used to them gradually. I would throw in a few toys to encourage them to go in.

Once the girls were okay wandering in and out of the crates, I put towels in them so they could have a lie down. I would also give them filled kongs to enjoy in there. I began to enclose them by putting puppy fencing across the entrances and holding it in place with five litre bottles of water. I did this for short periods, then gradually increasing the time.

I made four thick cushions to fit the crates so the girls would be comfortable on their long journey. Then the doors were fitted and the girls began to have their meals inside their crates and learnt to be left alone while I went out.

I was able to buy four special nozzles to

covered the windows to make it dark and put on the air conditioner to make it cold to simulate the cargo hold of the plane.

Two weeks before we left, I put the girls in their crates at midnight, alone, and in the dark. Of course, they howled, whined and barked as they had slept with me since I first brought them home. But I had to do this for their sake.

I let them out at 6 am the following morning. The next night they went to bed at 11, then 10, 9, 8, 7 and finally the night before we left – 6 pm and they were fine the next morning at 6 am. At this point, I knew they were prepared for a 12 hour flight. There was nothing more I could do.

Leaving Malaysia

We drove to Kuala Lumpur International Airport and met our vet there. He had all the paperwork signed and stayed with the girls until they were loaded onto the plane.

At 4 pm, we had to leave them locked in their crates in a room. It was the hardest thing I have ever done. I cried all the way back home.

We finished packing and waited for the taxi to take us back to the airport. Once there, we nervously waited to hear from our vet that the girls were safely onboard and then we boarded the plane and left Malaysia.

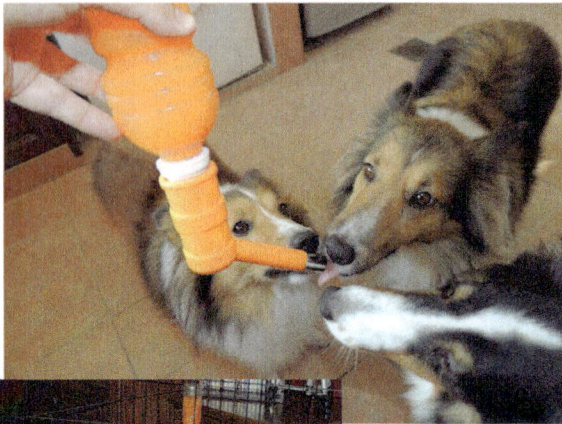

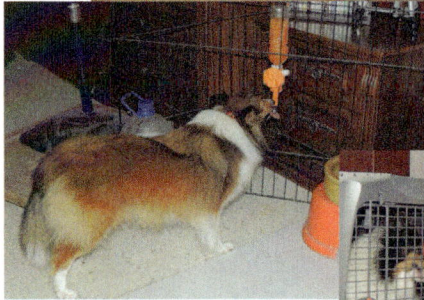

fit any plastic water bottle. To teach the girls to drink from these I filled a bottle with carrot juice as they love carrots. I also smeared peanut butter on the nozzle to tempt them. They soon got the hang of it as they were very clever shelties!

I attached a bottle to a piece of puppy fencing placed near the water bowl so they could get a drink whenever they wanted. Next, the bottles were attached to the doors of the crates and gradually over time I watered the carrot juice down until they would drink just water. Now I knew they would be okay for drinks on the flight.

Then came the most difficult stage for all of us. I moved their crates into a spare bedroom,

Arrival In The UK

We arrived at Heathrow 5:30 am. As soon as we got our luggage we went straight round to the Animal Quarantine Centre. The lady on the desk informed us that the four shelties from Malaysia were 'absolutely fine' with 'no problems at all'... oh what a relief to hear those words! We waited for a few hours while vet checks and documents were processed.

Then finally, the moment we longed for. The door opened and our four little girls came out to meet us!

Fortunately, because all of the girls had undergone many blood tests, vaccinations and other treatments before leaving Malaysia, they did not have to stay in quarantine on arrival at Heathrow and were allowed to enter the UK after only a few hours.

They were so happy, dancing around, tails wagging, lots of licks and kisses. Enya must have made friends with the staff because she tried to go back inside again!

Eventually, we took our girls and our luggage outside to the waiting pet taxi and loaded everything into it. The crates had to be dismantled and stacked on top of the dog cage. The girls were put into two cage areas where they slept all the way home. Once they had explored their new garden and house, had lots to drink and a nice dinner, they all climbed onto my bed and crashed out, four jetlagged shelties!

The next day we had a nice walk to the local river and we enjoyed the relief knowing we had done it after months of stress and hard work. They were all safely in England, ready to start a new life in the country in Lincolnshire where the girls could get used to a very different climate and experience seasons such as spring, autumn and snowy winters instead of those year long 'tropical summers'!

Now Enya, Glory and Gracie are nine years old and Blossom is fifteen soon to be 16. They have enjoyed a very adventurous and happy life together and have made my own life complete.

Onyx, Drifter and Skye at Latrigg Lake District UK

Photographs and story by Linda Bolt

WEE CHARLIE BOUNCES BACK

Charlie's story from the 2021 annual continues as he spent the last year fighting an unknown illness after eating some grass.

🐾 🐾
🐾 🐾

I have had some health problems in April this year. I was very ill, after eating some grass in a local park. I developed constant hiccups and my body was trembling. My pawrents took me straight to the vet. They thought I had eaten something in the grass but were not sure what it was. I got an injection to settle my stomach and some pain relief.

Things slightly improved but we were back and forth to the vet for two weeks and blood work done twice. Both times the results came back normal which baffled our vets, nothing was showing up. My pawrents knew something was still wrong so I had a scan on my abdomen. The scan revealed that my gallbladder had a lot of slow-moving sludge that could explain why I was ill.

Shetland Sheepdogs are at a predisposition to developing a Gallbladder Mucoceles (GBM). It is characterised by distension of the gallbladder by a thick mass of sludge and mucus (rather than liquid bile) and may result in obstruction and rupture of the gallbladder which can be fatal if untreated. Symptoms of this include vomiting, loss of appetite and abdominal pain and discomfort.

Because of this my pawrents and vet decided I should be seen by a specialist vet in this field. I was referred to a specialist team of vets at a veterinary hospital in Glasgow. My pawrents were so worried about me but I knew they would take good care of me. I had various tests and scans done at the veterinary hospital, it was an anxious four hour wait for my pawrents. The specialist vet found that I do have gallbladder sludge. The good news was the gallbladder itself looked healthy. There was no thickening of the wall lining, all bile ducts are healthy, no blockages, the sludge is mobile and

not thick and no sign of a Gallbladder Mucocele.
What they did find was my pancreas was inflamed and this was more than likely to have been the cause of me being so very ill. I have been diagnosed with pancreatitis. I am now on a supplement for this and a low-fat diet, so no more sausages for me! Because I do have this sludge in the gallbladder the vet has advised to scan every 3-4 months to keep an eye on it.

Since being on my new low-fat diet I have had no more relapses. I'm back to enjoying my adventures out over the hills and frisbee fun on the beach. I am so lucky to have the best pawrents in the world who look after me so well. They make sure I have the best life filled with lots of fun, but most of all lots of love as all us beautiful shelties deserve.

Lots of love to you all from Wee Charlie xxx

Story by Lana Robinson

A LINE OF CHAMPIONS

Lana Robinson reflects on what has helped her create a massively successful line of champion show dogs and looks towards the future of her Lavika breed line

🐾 | 🐾 🐾 🐾 🐾 🐾
🐾 | 🐾 🐾 🐾 🐾 🐾

I started showing in the UK show ring 12 years ago. To date we have made seven champions and five more Lavika shelties are on two CCs which means they need one more win to gain their crown.

My first champion CH MILESEND GOODTIMES OF LAVIKA is now 13 and still looking amazing. Her daughter is CH LAVIKA SUMMER TIME, her son is CH LAVIKA LUMINARY and her grandchildren are CH LAVIKA LIFE TIME and CH LAVIKA GOOD LUCK.

I am also very proud of my boys CH JAPARO MIDNIGHT STORM AT LAVIKA and CH SHELLRICKS YOU MAY ME LUCK, who not only won their titles, but played a grand role in breeding not just of my dogs but all over the world.

While there is no one perfect sheltie, when I look at my dogs I always smile as I like what I see. For me, they are my perfect shelties.

I plan to carry on with the same type, same line, same qualities and same success. I love shelties of all colours, but sables seem to be my favourites at the moment. My daughter Katya Robinson, who is also holding the LAVIKA prefix, started her own line which is tricolour and blue merles. They are very similar in breeding, line and type, she is planning to carry on with her young line too.

Knowledge, practice, skills and talent are all important. Learning, practising, putting a lot of time and effort into your hobby brings you joy and happiness. The next step is to use your knowledge and make your decisions wisely.

Love your dogs, they bloom in a happy environment.

A SHELTIE FOR ALL SEASONS

We all know how photogenic shelties can be at any time of year. In this edition we've gathered together some of the most spectacular shots of our sheltie friends enjoying seasonal weather around the globe. I'm sure you can agree that a sheltie by your side looks good in all weathers!

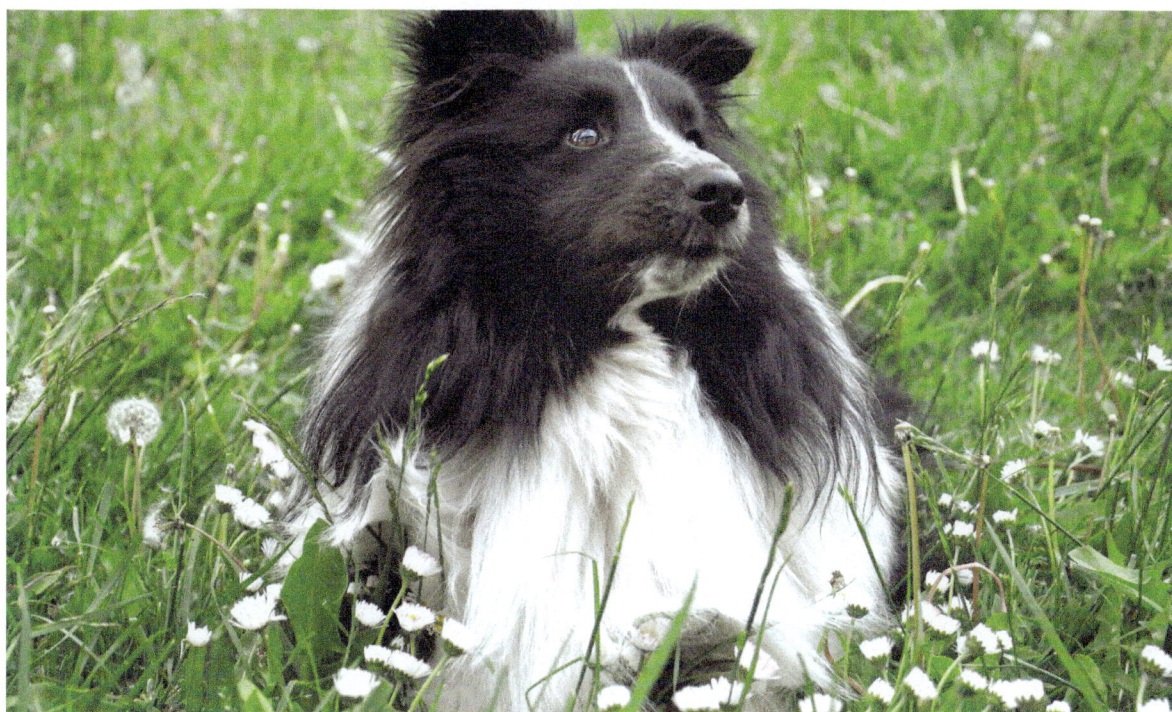

Oreo is 15 months old, from Hungary and feels fresh as a daisy!

Facing page: Keeko, 6 from Arbroath, Angus, Scotland among the cherry blossom

Above: Bryn, Charli and Jordie from New Zealand are pretty in the daffodils

Below: Teddy, Talia and Mia in the bluebells in Norfolk, UK

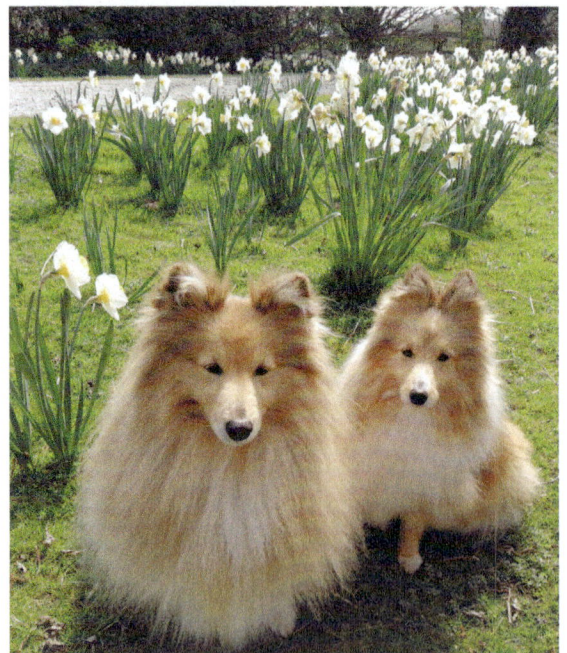

Saphie and Elsa enjoying the daffodils in Norfolk, UK

Top Right: Aline our cover star, 8 from Hungary looks spectacular in the spring flowers

Right: Amigo, 4 from Nørresø, Denmark looks majestic in the wildflowers

Bottom Right: Mila Flo and Pearl hiding in the poppies in the UK

Above L to R: Lexi, 1 from Bristol, UK on a summer adventure, Roxy, 12.5 enjoying a summer wind in Norfolk, UK and Keeko, 6 from Arbroath, Angus, Scotland on a beach trip.

Below: Teddy and Talia having some summer loving in Norfolk, UK

Facing page clockwise from top left: Bernie, 6 months is sailing on a summer day, Saphie and Elsa keeping cool in the shade in Norfolk UK, Ben, 4, Bramble, 7 and Rosie, 2 enjoying a day by the seaside from Norfolk, UK and Aline, 8 from Hungary jumping for joy in the summer sun.

Clockwise from top left: Spiggie, 2 from Suffolk UK cooling down from the summer heat in a paddling pool, Reglisse, 1 enjoying the summer flowers in a Park, Les Pavillons sous Bois, France, Cali, 3 catching some zzzz's in Berkshire, UK and Leone, 2, breathing in the summer air in Ottawa, Ontario.

Above: Cali, 3 in an autumnal sunset in Berkshire, UK.

Far left: Keeko, 6 from Arbroath, Angus, Scotland in the autumn leaves.

Left: Mila, Flo and Pearl trying to keep clean in their coats on a very muddy walk in the UK!

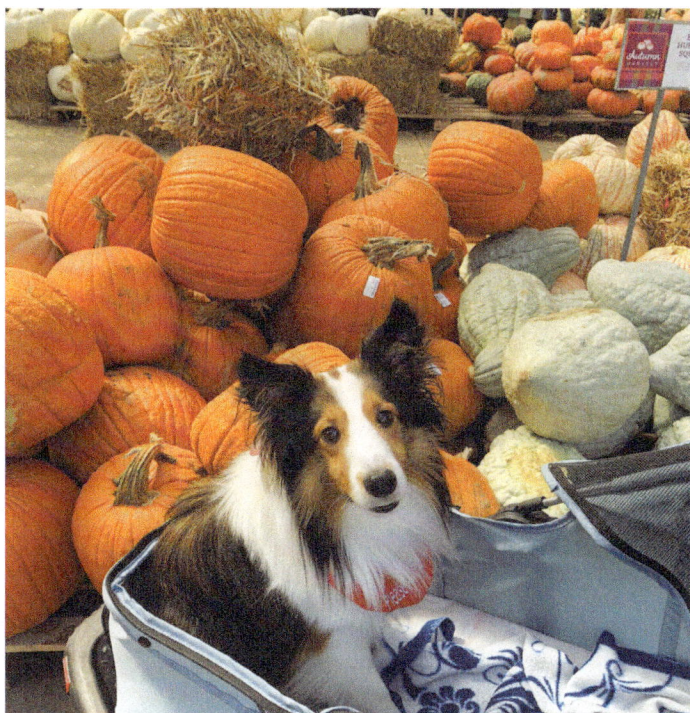

Chip, 2, picking out the best pumpkin in Fort Worth, Texas

Ernesto, 1, on an autumnal walk with his dad outside of London, UK

Pixel, 2 and Reglisse 1, playing in the autumn sun in the Bondy Forest, France

Left: Wee Charlie in Scotland and right: Saphie and Elsa on a muddy walk in Norfolk UK. Below: Apricot amongst the pumpkins in Denmark.

Mia, 6, bathed in golden light in Norfolk, UK

Clockwise from top: Aline, 8 from Hungary looking striking against autumnal reds, Bryn in the autumn leaves in New Zealand and Spiggie, 2 from Suffolk UK posing in the forest

Clockwise from top: Alfie, 9 from Hunstanton, Norfolk, Leone, 2 from Ottawa, Ontario, Malchy, 6 from East Anglia, UK and Smudge, 1 from Ipswich, UK

Facing page: Bryn, Charli and Jordie against a stunning New Zealand landscape

Above: Mila, Flo and Pearl from the UK

Clockwise from top left: Joy, 2 from Norfolk UK, Lexi, 1 from Bristol, UK, Toby, 5 from Maryland, USA, Ernesto, 1 from London, UK, and Ben, 4, Bramble, 7 and Rosie 2 from Norfolk, UK

Cali, 3 from Berkshire, UK wants to know if you'd like to build a snowman with her?

Jordie from New Zealand

Pixel, 2 and Reglisse, 1 playing in their garden in France

Above L to R: Bryn from New Zealand, Teddy, 11 from Apple Valley, Minnesota, USA and Wee Charlie from Scotland

Clockwise from left: Teddy, 2 and Mia, 6 from Norfolk, UK, Spiggie, 2 from Suffolk UK, Boo from Raleigh, North Carolina, USA, Talia, 2 from Norfolk, UK and Champ from Raleigh, North Carolina, USA

Left: Alfie, 9 and Annie, 11 from Hunstanton, Norfolk

Bottom Left: Keeko, 6 from Arbroath, Angus, Scotland and bottom right: Aline, 8, from Hungary

A VERY SHELTIE CHRISTMAS

L to R: Lexi, 1 from Bristol, UK, Teddy, 1 and Sonny, 4 months in the UK, Talia, 2, Mia 6 and Teddy, 3 from Norfolk, UK and Wee Charlie from Scotland

Chip, 2 from Fort Worth, Texas

Echo and Encore in Centerville, Ohio, USA

Right: Santa Joy and her trusty reindeer Grace from Norfolk UK and far right: Saphie and Elsa from Norfolk UK

L to R: Toby, 5 from Maryland in the USA, Amigo, 3 wasn't impressed with his mum's idea for a photoshoot and Teddy, 11 from Apple Valley, Minnesota

Above: Glory, Gracie, Enya and Blossom the Malaysian sheltie girls enjoying christmas in Lincolnshire and above right: Cali, 3 from Berkshire, UK

Malchy, 6 from East Anglia

Gracie from Lincolnshire was only allowed to go outside and play in the snow if she wore her hat and scarf. Looking very fetching Gracie!

Lacey, 11, Gibbs, 5 on the bench, Tripp, 3 months in the box and Willie, 10 on the ground from Berkeley Springs, West Virginia, USA

Lucy, 9 from Harrisburg, North Carolina, USA

Griffin woke me up at 3 am on a Saturday morning vomiting. He vomited five times between 3-8 am. I remember thinking… why does this always happen on a weekend? I called my vet and made an appointment. They took the conservative approach and gave him fluids and anti-nausea medicine.

This is a routine treatment for initial vomiting, but little did we know that this was not a routine situation.

By Sunday Griffin refused to eat and was not drinking water. His temperature was 103.9°F (39.9°C). He became increasingly lazy over the day and hid in the corner of our bathroom – completely unlike him at eleven months old. He is always very active and eats well.

I took him to the emergency vet on Sunday at 5 pm and he was finally seen at 9 pm! He had an x-ray to rule out a blockage, blood tests, was given fluids and started on IV Metronidazole, a common drug used for gastrointestinal disorders.
The emergency vet thought he was fighting an infection somewhere in his abdominal area.

On Monday morning we

GRIFFIN'S CONQUEST

A Puppy's Conquest of a Pancreatic Abscess

transferred him to our regular vet, they continued the treatment and he spent all day Monday and Tuesday at our vet. We were able to take him home Tuesday evening and by Wednesday he seemed much better.

However, he woke me up Thursday at 4 am vomiting again. My gut instinct told me that the symptoms—not the cause—were being treated by the vets who had seen him.

For many years I have relied on the Virginia-Maryland College of Veterinary Medicine for speciality care (hereafter referred to as VT).

I have donated to them for many years because they have helped so many of my shelties and cats. I called VT, told them the situation and that I was bringing him in as an emergency.

I also called my usual vet and told them to send all of his records to VT. We live more than two hours from VT and arrived at 10:45 am. They admitted Griffin for tests including blood work, an ultrasound and samples for cultures. They called me at 4:30 pm and said that he had some type of abscess in the abdominal area, but the cultures (aspirates) did not

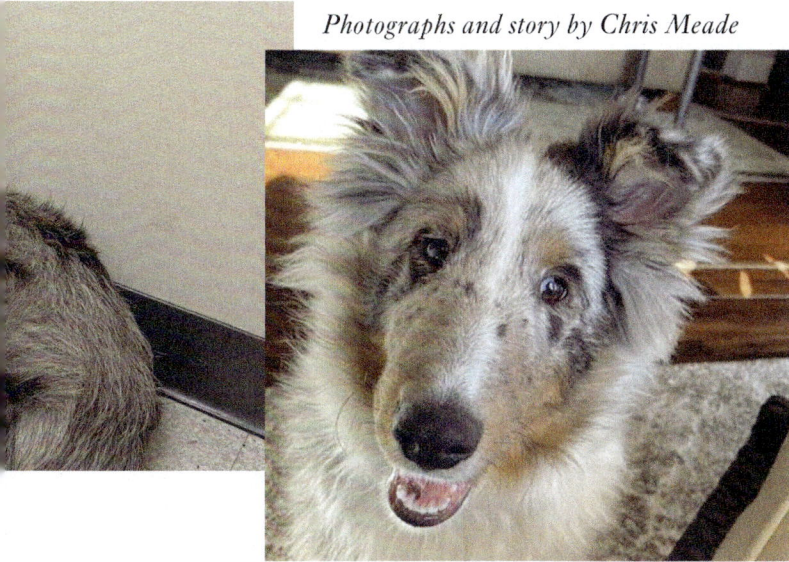

Photographs and story by Chris Meade

" *His surgeon, Dr Otto Lanz, said in his 30+ years of surgery he had never seen a pancreatic abscess in an 11-month old puppy and they could find no reason for the abscess.*

reveal a definitive diagnosis.

He needed an exploratory laparotomy to find out the problem. Little did I know at the time that 50–86% of dogs with pancreatic abscesses do not survive the surgery. I found this out after he had the surgery when doing a review of Veterinary Journals.

He had surgery Friday morning and a 7x8cm abscess involving the majority of the right limb of the pancreas was found. A significant amount of adhesion was found involving abdominal organs. The adhesions were manually broken down. A large amount

of caseous material was suctioned from the opening of the abscess.

The remainder of the abdominal exploratory findings were unremarkable. The abdominal cavity was then copiously lavaged. A Jackson–Pratt drain was placed in the abscess and the tube was passed through the right side of the abdominal incision. There were, fortunately, no complications during surgery. His surgeon, Dr Otto Lanz, said in his 30+ years of surgery he had never seen a pancreatic abscess in an 11-month old puppy and they could find no reason for

the abscess. Griffin had not eaten anything that caused it either because they found no markings in either the intestine or colon to indicate a puncture.

We picked up Griffin the following Monday and had strict orders to keep him quiet. He wore a surgery suit so he could not have access to his incision which stretched from his neck to his anal area. We separated him from our other three shelties.

He was eating and all seemed well, until Thursday when he started vomiting again. His temperature was 104.1°F (40°C) and I panicked.

I called VT and told them what was happening. They said to bring him in and we arrived at 1:45 am. He vomited three times in the car and by the time we arrived at VT his temperature was 104.8°F (40.4°C). They admitted him, started fluids, pain medicine and various nausea drugs.

In the morning, they told me they would be doing a CT scan to determine the problem. After talking with

the Radiology Department, they decided to do a repeat ultrasound first to see if anything had changed from his first ultrasound. If they saw no changes, they would proceed to the CT scan.

Around noon, The Chief of ER/ICU called me and said they had found an ulcer in his duodenum that was most likely caused by the Rimadyl he was taking for pain post-surgery and/or a combination of the Rimadyl and surgery he had. It was causing extreme pain and vomiting.

They began to treat the ulcer, his severe abdominal pain and nausea. He would not eat anything and on Sunday they told me if he did not start eating, they would have to put in a feeding tube.

At the suggestion of a friend, I used Instacart to send him some grilled chicken that he loves. As I was too far away to deliver it, a shopper picked up the chicken and delivered it to VT. As soon as he smelt it, he started eating. Success!

On Monday morning, they called to say he could come home so my husband and I picked him up. Again, he was eating and not vomiting. But by Wednesday,

he was hiding in the corner again and his temp was 103.8°F (39.8°C). The difference this time is that he was not vomiting and was eating, so I knew it was not the same thing as the other two incidents. You can't imagine how frustrating this was!

I first called VT and was told the vets who originally cared for him were on vacation. I then called my trusted vet (she had been on vacation when this started with Griffin, so another vet in the practice saw him). She said to re-take his temperature at noon and if it was still high I should bring him in.

I took him in and we discussed putting him on antibiotics. He did not have a planned antibiotic regimen after his surgery, because the

cultures did not show any bacteria. But both my trusted vet and I sensed that he had an infection somewhere that had not been cultured or had developed after the surgery.

He was given two injections of Baytril (Enrofloxacin) in the vet's office and then put on oral antibiotics for another ten days. Luckily he showed major improvement within 48 hours and is now happily on the way to a full recovery!

We suspect that Griffin's case will be presented to many aspiring veterinary students in VT's classes as it is a unique case. All that we care about is that he is alive, thriving and doing all the normal things that sheltie puppies do!

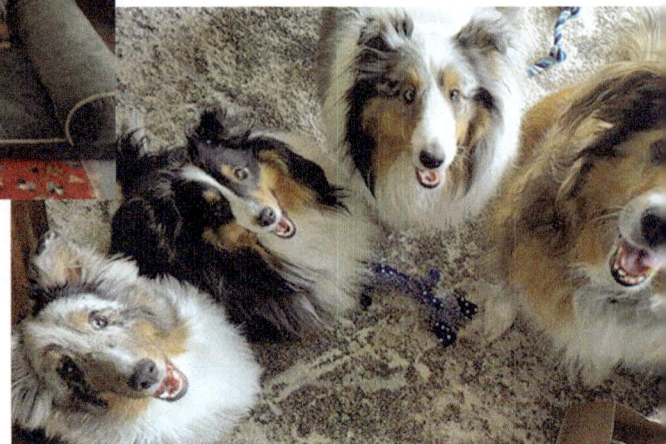

Netty Nan's
TUNA CAKE

Our favourite high value treat!

Here's a great recipe courtesy of Netty Nan (from Shelties By The Sea) to make your very own tuna cake. Only a few ingredients needed and you can add some optional extras to make it even more special. Great cubed as a high value training treat or for barkday celebrations in funky shapes like we did!

Ingredients

Tin of tuna chunks

1 egg

Plain flour to bind

A splash of water

Grated carrot (optional)

Cheese grated or in chunks (optional)

Kibble (optional)

Beaten egg to glaze

Kibble or biscuits to decorate

Method

Mix the egg and tuna and then add flour slowly to bind until it's a sticky dough. If it becomes too dry add a splash of water to loosen it up.

Add any extra optional flavourings like cheese, carrot or kibble at this point – be creative!

Spoon into a cake or loaf tin or silicone moulds of choice. Add any biscuits or kibble decorations and glaze with a beaten egg.

Bake for approximately 25 minutes at 180 ° G or until golden brown.

Angel was born a singleton by C section on 1st November 2005, the longed-for female to continue the Torriglen line. The birth was at a very sad time for me as I had recently lost Jamie, my much-loved boy, who had died suddenly seventeen days after gaining his agility title.

Inca, Angel's mum doted on her baby but wasn't producing very much milk. The first alert to this was when I checked on the whelping box to find the pair seemingly sleeping. Inca stepped out of the bed, but the puppy didn't move. I reached inside and to my horror she was cold and very dehydrated. I set about rubbing her in a towel to warm her up. She was alive but very sluggish. I called the vet and set off with them both, Angel on a hot water bottle and Inca looking very anxious beside her.

Angel was given something to hydrate her and Inca was injected with Oxytocin to try to bring the milk down. I also mentioned I had never seen signs of her defecating. Humouring me the vet said "the mother will be keeping her clean, it is unlikely you will see anything." I explained that I had observed this many times before and that I knew when a mum has performed this duty. At

Story by Louise Saunders

ANGEL'S MIGHT

that point, the vet checked Angel's temperature. When he removed the thermometer, it was tipped with the sticky black meconium. I had been right; she had passed nothing.

We returned home with some milk substitute to supplement her feeding and I hoped everything would be alright. Inca's milk didn't improve much so the supplementary feeding continued until weaning. Angel was still losing weight but after a week she was back to her birth weight and some weeks later we thought our problems were behind us. She was weaned as early as possible and she was doing well. A happy, normal pup full of

mischief.

One day while she was running around, she starting spluttering and bringing up clear fluid. This occurred on several occasions. During these episodes, she seemed quite distressed so we returned to the vet, who prescribed antibiotics which did the trick. The same problem happened again a few weeks later and more antibiotics were given.

Shortly after the second antibiotic, her last puppy vaccine was due and it was on this visit to the vet a health check revealed that Angel had developed a significant heart murmur. This didn't appear

> **As I think of Angel I remember her tremendous courage and determination.**
>
> Louise Saunders

to bother or hinder her in any way and she continued to develop as normal until one day I noticed her gait was a little odd, particularly from behind. I feared maybe it was hip dysplasia but over the next few months, there was clearly something wrong in all four legs. Her front legs were splaying from the knees and she would often stagger and cry out in pain.

The next vet visit was to a specialist. X-rays revealed the lower bones in all four legs were of different lengths. The front inside bones, longer than the outer causing the splaying. A similar thing was happening at the back, putting pressure on her patella's. Nothing could be done except offer pain relief.

My husband and I discussed whether it would be kinder to have her put to sleep but despite all her problems, Angel was a happy pup, definitely one of the gang and unaware she was any different.

As she grew, she attended training classes. She passed all her class tests, bronze and silver Road Safety and Good Citizen tests. She came to all the shows with my other shelties, loved camping and caravanning and even did her bit raising money in a sponsored down-stay for sheltie rescue.

When I look back at the nine and a half years of Angel's life. She came to me when I was in deep despair. Her needs forced me to stop wallowing. She always demonstrated strength of character, always cheerful, never did she curl a lip or snap. Everybody who knew her loved her. She truly was an Angel.

❤ HEART DOGS

There are always those special dogs that hold a place in our heart. We call these our 'heart dogs'. It doesn't matter how much time, space or shelties lie between us, on these pages we celebrate the ones that have left paw prints on our hearts forever.

Buddy

Pam Marshall's said of Buddy, 'he came to me at one year old as his previous owners couldn't contain him (!) So funny and happy, this little man was always wagging his tail. I sadly lost him in 2020 at nine years, far too soon'.

Sky

'Sky came to me at five years old. I was his fifth home which was unbelievable to me as he was the sweetest, gentlest little boy ever. I lost him in 2018, about two weeks after this photo was taken at 14 years old'. – Pam Marshall

Spice

Spice was Barbara Slack's heart dog, aged about seven in this photo, from Milnrow near Rochdale, UK.

Roxy

Denise Burton from Norfolk UK says, 'Roxy (12.5 years old) came to me when I was feeling low and has helped pick me up so many times. She is my friend, companion, therapist, comedian and all-round beautiful little girl. She is such a strong and tough little old lady and survived major leg surgery this year'.

SHELTIES ON STAYCATION

The COVID-19 pandemic put much of the world into lockdown and even today we're experiencing various levels of 'normality'. In the UK with foreign travel out of the equation, as a nation in the past year we were encouraged to go on 'staycations' inside the UK to support our local economies until we were able to travel abroad more easily once again. Over the next few pages you can see a few of our favourite sheltie staycations that people have sent to us!

Archie and Rolo holidayed in North Wales over summer in a campervan!

Dice (8, tricolour) is uncle to Pandora (aka Panda, 6 blue merle). We live a long way from the seaside, in Newmarket, Suffolk. Panda absolutely LOVES the sea, but Dice hates water! However, we try to get there as often as we can and here are some photos of our last visit.

SHELTIES BY THE SEASIDE

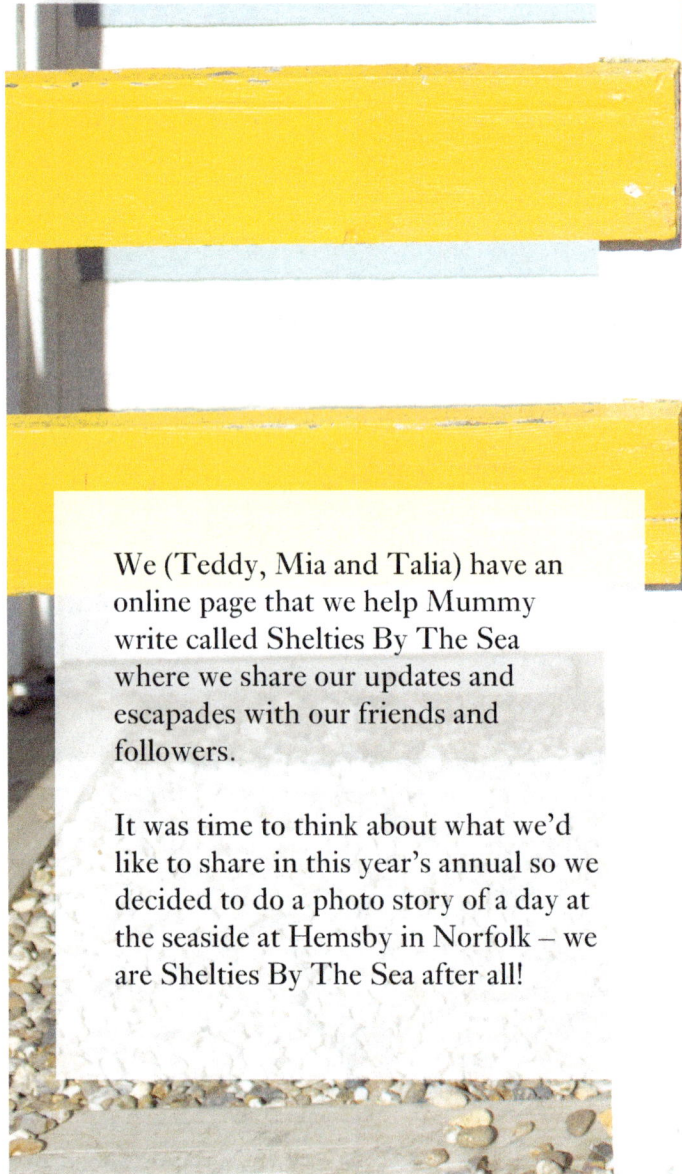

We (Teddy, Mia and Talia) have an online page that we help Mummy write called Shelties By The Sea where we share our updates and escapades with our friends and followers.

It was time to think about what we'd like to share in this year's annual so we decided to do a photo story of a day at the seaside at Hemsby in Norfolk – we are Shelties By The Sea after all!

" *I loved the beach hut and couldn't wait to show off my 'paws up' trick. I think we should buy our own beach hut to stash our treats!*

Teddy

Seaside Wonderland

We thought we had stepped into wonderland when we arrived. There was a giant bucket and spade and two giant deck chairs. Did someone shrink us shelties in the wash?

🐾 🐾

Riding High

We tried out some of the amusement rides. Mia especially liked her hot air balloon, she said she would like to float away from us and get some peace and quiet!

I lost track of the girls for a while. I saw the PAW Patrol ride and fancied having a go at riding a fire engine. Don't I look dashing in the hat? Guess I better go find those girls though…

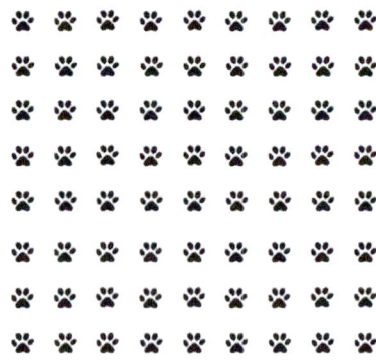

Teddy To The Rescue

Oh woof! How did you girls end up in there?! Don't worry, I'll get you out in a flash!

Slot Machine Saviours

Mummy and Netty Nan kept losing all their coins in the funny machines and the coins didn't come back. Don't worry, we put a stop to that! We know those coins are meant to pay for treats to go in our bellies, not to the mean coin eating machines!

Beach Time!

Choosing buckets and spades for the beach is serious business you know!

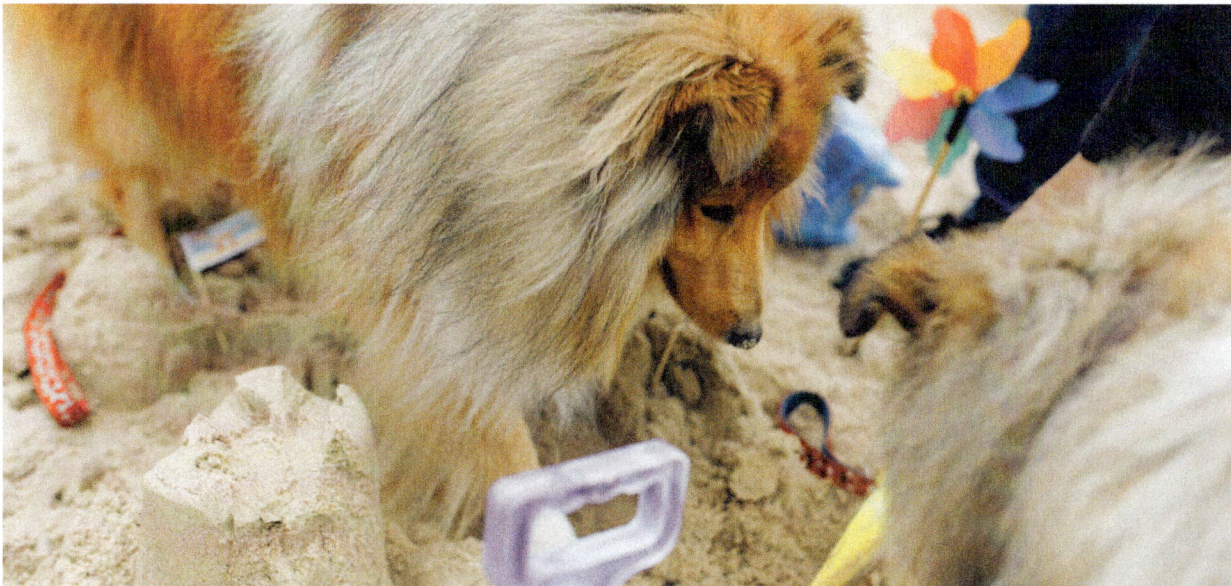

A Storm is Brewing!

We were getting tired after all that play time and Mummy saw some dark clouds on the horizon so said it was time to go home and finish off the day with a special surprise...

A Sweet End to a Great Day

No seaside visit would be complete without an ice cream and Netty Nan found us a pot of special doggie ice cream to take home with us. We tested it thorougly and give it all paws up!

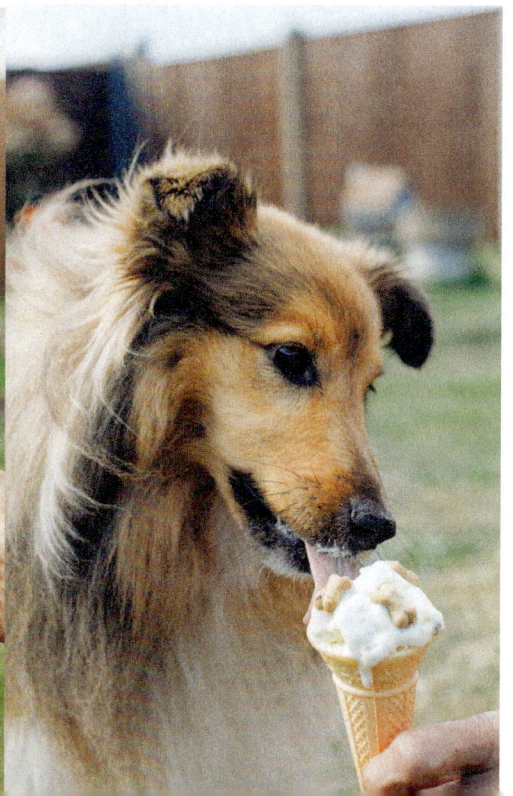

Rainbow Bridge

These are always the hardest pages to put together but it is a privilege to be able to honour these special souls that have crossed over to rainbow bridge. Until we meet again sweet shelties, run happy, run free.

Annie 24.09.09 – 15.09.21

It has been the worse week possible, the day we all dread. I am heartbroken to have lost my beautiful girl 'Annie' – Samhaven Magic Kiss at Karlaina ShCM.

She bounced into our life at nine weeks old. The Rough Collies (who loved her) wondered who was this little dynamo flying around the house. She was full of life and fun and we are truly grateful to have known and loved her so much, she was such a special girl to us both.

She had lots of successes in the show ring qualifying for Crufts many times over and gaining her stud book number. At open shows she won many BOB's (Best of Breed) and group wins culminating in winning her 'Show Certificate of Merit'. She even won BOB the day I retired her from the show ring as a veteran. The entries at these open shows she attended often had a champion or two entered so it was no mean feat. One of the highlights of her show career was winning Best in Show at the ECSSC breed club open show.

Outside of the show ring Annie excelled in toy unstuffing and throwing, football, inspecting the greenhouse, pea picking (and eating), noise making, neighbourhood watch and sous chef in the kitchen.

Thank you to Alison and Emma for letting me have her all those years ago. Sleep tight baby girl, my heart is breaking.

By Karen Smith

Kyloe Piper who was Crufts Prizewinner and worked Test 'C' only obedience.

My boy Archie (tricolour) with his best friend Rolo. Archie sadly passed in 2020 aged 12 and Rolo is now 7 and has a new friend Bernie who was born March 10th 2020, one week after Archie passed. I think Archie sent Bernie to me to mend a broken heart.

Flash went over to rainbow bridge age 14 on 20th March 2021 from Scalloway, Shetland.

❀ ❀ ❀ ❀ ❀ ❀ ❀ ❀ ❀

❀ ❀ ❀ ❀ ❀ ❀ ❀ ❀ ❀ ❀ ❀ ❀ ❀ ❀ ❀ ❀ ❀ ❀ ❀ ❀

My heart dog Maestro, who has gone to the bridge, but was my everything. From Centerville, Ohio, USA.

Willow went to rainbow bridge on July 14th 2021, just before her eleventh birthday. She was owned and loved by Lynne Stanley and all the family and is missed every single day. Willow was Lynne's last sheltie after forty four years of proud sheltie ownership.

Ash was 13 years old and we lost him sadly in July, Cambridgeshire UK. We were so lucky to have had a pup (Badger) reserved in a litter before we knew Ash was so ill.

❀ ❀ ❀ ❀ ❀ ❀ ❀ ❀ ❀ ❀ ❀ ❀ ❀ ❀ ❀ ❀ ❀ ❀ ❀

MINTY, LIGHTNING LASS   23/11/11 – 29/ 9/20

Minty, a thunderbolt of joy in living with a paw in everybody's business. Dear daughter of Beauly (centre) adored Mum of Daisy (L), Skye & Boppan and best friend to brother Wee Charlie. She flashed into our lives and lit up every minute of her nine years.Alive in our hearts in Scotland by parents of Minty, Ena & Allan Edgar

Photographs and story by Jo Austin

TRIBUTE TO AN ANGEL

Angel was twelve years and ten months old when she passed away on 22nd March 2021 in Hampshire, UK. She was my heart dog, my beautiful guardian angel and was featured in last years I Love Shelties Annual. This is my tribute to her...

"

Those who live alone with their shelties and those from families of all shapes and sizes feel the deep, unconditional love and the special connection and closeness that a sheltie brings to their lives.

Jo Austin

🐾 🐾
🐾 🐾
🐾 🐾

Writing about my journey with Angel has brought me many tears. As I recall our fondest moments as a family sharing our lives with such an amazing dog, it is hard not to be so deeply and profoundly moved by the enormous depth of love that so many felt for her. Her greatest achievements, happiest times and sad times are all engrained in our memories and will be cherished forever.

When Angel crossed over to the rainbow bridge she took a huge chunk of my heart with her. Some people say, 'she was just a dog'. I beg to differ! All those with a sheltie will agree with me when I say, 'they are family, they are our babies!' Those who live alone with their shelties and those from families of all shapes and sizes feel the deep, unconditional love and the special connection and closeness that a sheltie brings to their lives.

Angel was family, she was also my best friend, my soul mate and my guardian. She shared so much with me. She carried me through the darkest of times and celebrated with me during the happiest ones. She was always there. A solid, dependable presence. She never judged me. She loved me unconditionally with all her heart. I feel so privileged to have been loved by such a truly remarkable dog.

While there remains a huge void in my life but in my heart, I know that I am blessed to have Angel's granddaughter, Dory with me and there will be many more to join the ever-growing 'Calistros Sheltie Family'. Of that, I have no doubt. But you can not replace a dog. I can only hope that I can learn to live with the pain that accompanied her departure and offer the love that we shared to others. I think

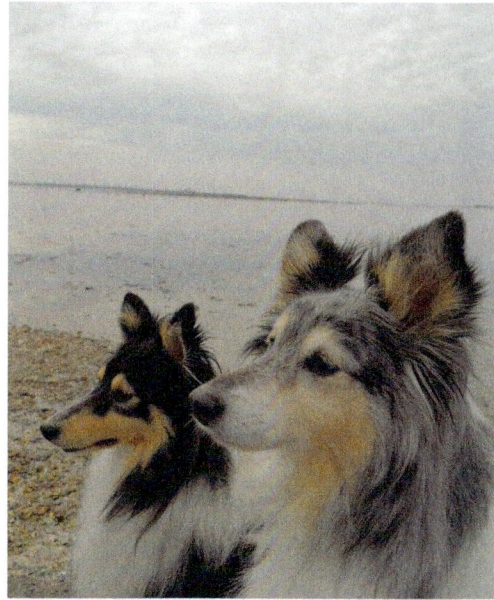

she would want that.

Angel was dearly loved so she departed this world with us present by her side reminding her of the deep love we felt for her right to the very end. I hope the last words she heard were me saying, 'I love you, Angel, I always have and always will!' I also apologised to her for the many times I got things wrong or just in case I ever failed her. She was very poorly. I like to think we set her free.

There have been many dark days since Angel left us. However, in the darkness, I'm reminded that I was blessed, that my family and friends were blessed and privileged to have shared our lives with such a truly magnificent, wonderful, loyal dog. We are all so deeply indebted to her and eternally grateful for the beautiful new lives and forever friends she gifted to us through her puppies and through her daughter, Millie's puppies.

No greater legacy could such a special dog have left us. So I will finish Angel's story with a message that was sent to me by the owner of one of her puppies.

'Angel founded a marvellous dynasty and sent threads of joy and companionship into the future'.

Angel, *Kelgrove Angel in Blue at Calistros.*

By Jo Austin

Bryn Charli and Jordie from New Zealand

RICHMAUS ORIGINS

In 1970, I was 18 years old and went along to *The One Man And His Dog Field Trials* with my uncle. It was there I spotted a sheltie and told my uncle I wanted one. My uncle's reply was, 'You'll just have to want. Don't go asking your father because the family can't afford one of those types of dogs'. *That's what they think*, I thought to myself.

Sometime later I found myself that long-awaited sheltie. I bought my first sheltie from a vicar and his wife from Sudbury costing me £35 (£555 in today's money) which was a real lot of money in the 70s. My boy's pedigree name was *Richmaus Captain Sensible* otherwise know as Thomas and he was the first sire I bred and I haven't stopped breeding since.

Over the years I have bred so many shelties, many of which have gone on to become champion dogs far and wide in France, Finland and Australia. Shelties I have bred have travelled all over the world to their forever homes – everywhere from France, Finland, Germany, Australia and Cyprus.

I'm still breeding at present and producing beautiful sheltie puppies and currently have eight shelties in total.

Top left: Maureen with Teddy, middle left: puppies from a recent litter, above left: Richmaus Captain Sensible and above right: current sire Navarrem Mr Sitges At Richmaus IKC (Teddy)

HERE COMES TROUBLE!

Shelties, what are they like?! We love them to bits but their curious nature sure gets them into a fix sometimes. Have a laugh at some of the funniest photos we received and see what this cheeky lot have been doing this year.

Cali has been playing in some puddles and got herself more than a bit muddy. Don't tell her a bath is waiting for her when she gets home!

Frosty decided no one needed to read the mail and is quite proud of his handiwork if he's being quite honest!

Badger caused a stink rolling in hedgehog poo and had to have his head washed!

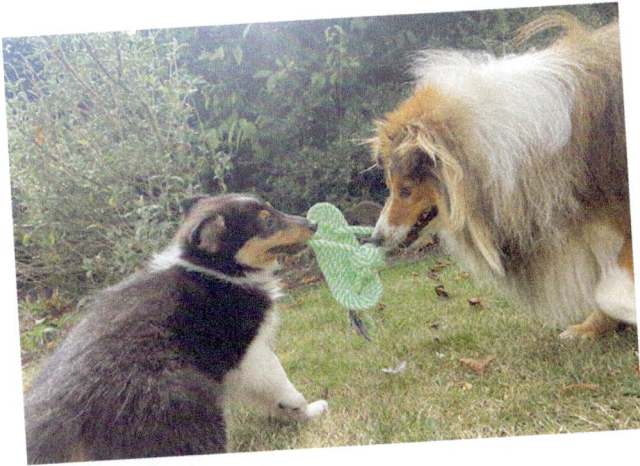

Smudge and puppy Kyle didn't
want to share while playing.
Wonder who won?!

Sonny and Teddy promise you they
are not discussing plans for world
domination. There's nothing to see
her mum, honest!

Laddie stole a
glove because
he thought
the sparkles
brought out his
eye colour!

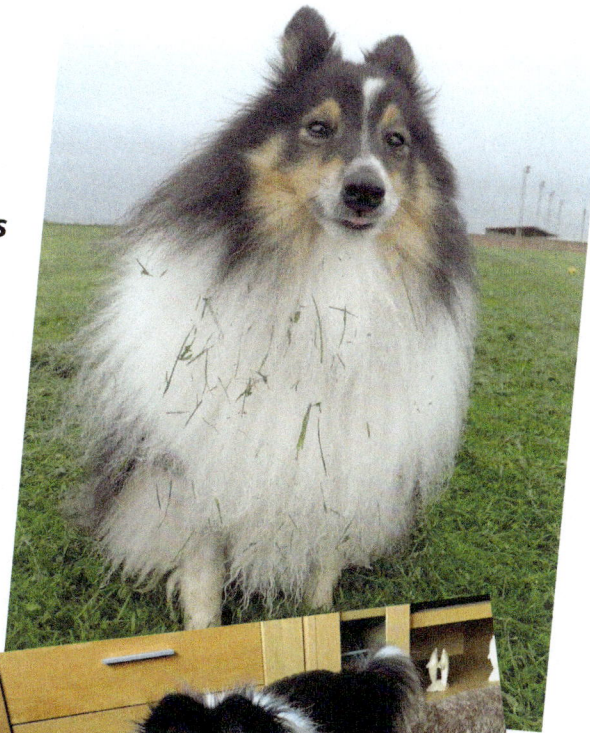

Keeko has been exceptionally
naughty with double trouble! Not
only is she a renowned sock thief
but she had just been brushed
before a walk when she decided
she needed a coating of freshly
cut grass on her. To add insult
to injury she then proceeded to
stick out her tongue at her mum.
Cheeky Keeko!

SPECIAL MENTIONS

Sometimes a story or picture really grabs our heart as we go through submissions and we want to include them even though they don't fit into the main photo/story categories. Here are a few of those very special shelties that deserve a special mention in our 2022 annual!

🐾 🐾

Ben and Kody are four year old brothers. Very sadly their owner Harry died suddenly in 2019 and this is a small tribute to him. Harry's sister Jean kindly took Ben and Kody to live with her in Essex and she adores the boys. They are very pampered shelties and go to the groomers every month. Don't they both look so handsome and happy? We're sure Harry is looking down on you all and thank you Jean for doing such a wonderful job looking after his beloved boys.

We loved hearing Gibbs' story. He is a 6 year old Therapy Dog. When the COVID lockdown started, he could no longer do visits, so his owner had a life size image made and took it to the nursing home for visits. This is Gibbs and his twin. Way to Gibbs!

🐾 🐾 🐾 🐾 🐾 🐾 🐾 🐾 🐾 🐾 🐾 🐾 🐾 🐾 🐾 🐾
🐾 🐾 🐾 🐾 🐾 🐾 🐾 🐾 🐾 🐾 🐾 🐾 🐾 🐾 🐾 🐾

The Sheltie That Started It All...

I was 18 when I got my first sheltie in 1968 after my dad died. Jaunty came into my life to help me get over the loss. I became interested in obedience and entered him in shows. Shortly after I married in 1973 Jaunty became very ill and went to Rainbow Bridge, aged five. I always say Jaunty was around to fill that gap between dad's death and getting married. He started my love of shelties.

Barbara Slack

🐾 🐾 🐾 🐾 🐾 🐾 🐾 🐾 🐾 🐾 🐾 🐾 🐾
🐾 🐾 🐾 🐾 🐾 🐾 🐾 🐾 🐾 🐾 🐾 🐾 🐾

Laddie is three from Greenwood, Arkansas USA and he is a sheltie mix. In fact, he is the first sheltie mix we've heard from so we simply had to include him in this year's annual – just look at that face!

His owner Amy says, 'he's a very special pup that came to me from an unwanted litter. We've had a bond since day one, I'm his person and he's my heart dog. He's always right there ready to go for an adventure.'

🐾 🐾

Hello to these gorgeous faces...

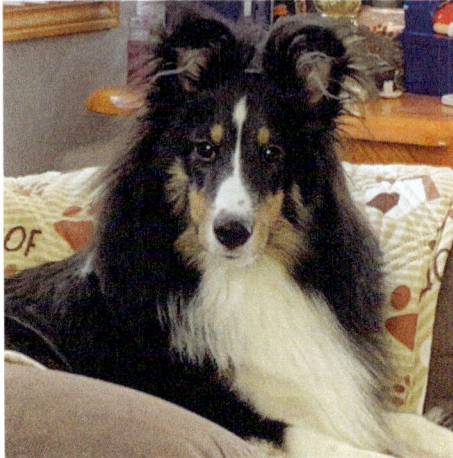

River is 3 from Elmhurst, Illinois, USA. Her owner Kathy says, 'She loves our grandsons and stands by the door and cries when they leave. As you know shelties are so smart. When the grandsons play tag outside, she chases them all over the yard. She immediately knew that the patio, wood chips and garage steps were safety zones and stops when they are on them and waits til they are on the grass again to chase them. We started out our love of shelties with Copper, a sable and when he died got Frosty, a blue merle. After Frosty's death we decided we needed to get a tri, so we got River'.

Fenstyle Sweet Bramble, is a seven year old tri sheltie and has had two litters of puppies. Ben is four years old and was from a litter of two and Rosie is two years old now. Both Ben and Rosie have stayed living with mum Bramble on the Norfolk coast, while Ben's brother Fraiser now lives on the Bournemouth coast with another family member. What an adorable family!

Left: This is Moth (man of the house) who is one from Cambridge. His owner Nikki says, 'He is confident, cheeky, ALWAYS happy and just the nicest dog to have the pleasure to own. We do agility which he loves and is learning quickly, he also loves little holidays all over the country in our caravan with me and his two older sisters (crossbreeds)'.

Right: Oreo is 15 months old living in Hungary. His owner Nóra says, 'Oreo is the most amazing dog I have ever had. He is clever and handsome, he is doing agility and we want to compete in this sport when he is old enough. We hike together, travel together, he knows a lot of tricks, he can sit, lay, stay, come, turn left, turn right, sit pretty, roll over, give a paw, go backwards, bow, do slalom between my legs, close a cabinet, put his toys away, jump in my arms, put his back legs on a balancing pillow'.

A Bit of Sheltie Therapy

We wanted to do an extra special shout out to Chip who is two living in Fort Worth, Texas with his mum Lynelle. Chip is in training to be a therapy dog which we think is absolutely pawsome. Good luck with training Chip and make sure to keep us updated!

Encore running in his first AKC Fast CAT trial from Centerville, Ohio.
BY MLBAER PHOTOGRAPHY

🐾 🐾 🐾 🐾 🐾 🐾 🐾 🐾 🐾 🐾 🐾 🐾 🐾 🐾 🐾 🐾

Lacey is Fighting On

This is PACH 2 Lacey, retired, from Berkeley Springs, West Virginia, USA. This photo was taken at an agility trial veteran run in May.

Her mum Sandy said, "The jump bars were on the floor, but she was still jumping 12 inches. She was my first agility dog. She was going to be my obedience champion but there was just one little problem, this high energy girlie hated obedience, so at 61 years old, I became an agility handler and never looked back.

Lacey was diagnosed with a mast cell tumor in July of 2020 but her surgery was successful with clean margins. In July of 2021, she was diagnosed with transitional cell carcinoma, TCC (bladder cancer). This is a cancer prevalent in shelties and several other breeds.

We have chosen to just keep her comfortable and pain free, no chemo, surgery or radiation. She is still the feisty alpha girlie and keeps her three brothers on their best behaviour. Our motto is 'live life to the fullest, one day at a time'."

😺😺😺😺😺😺😺😺😺😺😺😺😺😺😺😺😺
😺😺😺😺😺😺😺😺😺😺😺😺😺😺😺😺😺
😺😺😺😺😺😺😺😺😺😺😺😺😺😺😺😺

Honouring Anya

This is Anya, rescued at age eighteen months from a local rescue centre, unwanted due to having a heart murmer. She became the sweetest, most beautiful soul inside and out, a best friend and loved by many. Sadly journeyed over rainbow bridge aged eight years and ten months after losing a well fought battle against cancer. The most amazing girl who is much missed by 'Sam' (Sandra) Hime.

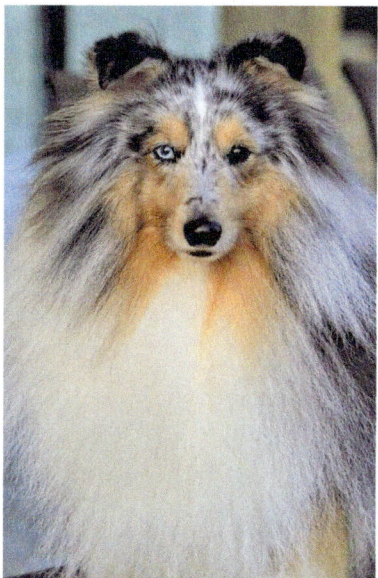

The Rarest of Them All

Meet this beautiful blue boy Lincoln, Tiakina Truly Madly Deeply who is four. His owner Allison says, 'Lincoln is an extremely rare sheltie as he hardly ever barks! How we managed to be so lucky to get a Ssheltie that doesn't bark I don't know, but our other shelties certainly make up for Lincoln's silence'. We're certainly truly, madly and deeply in love with that handsome face!

😺😺😺😺😺😺
😺😺😺😺😺😺
😺😺😺😺😺😺

We simply had to share this incredible photo of stunning scenery in Denmark to match the stunning shelties in the foreground! L to R: Artemis, Amigo, Silver, Aisee and Sesse with Hammershus in the background, Bornholm Denmark Ages from 4–11 years old (Kennel Sheltiedream, Denmark).

MAJESTICALLY WINDSWEPT

There's something about a sheltie standing with their coat blowing in the wind that is simply majestic, I'm sure you'll agree. Here's a few of our favourite submissions showing off that gorgeous coat blowing in the wind.

L to R: Carly, Saphie and Elsa.

Bottom L to R: Bryn, Charli and Jordie and Leone

L to R: Onyx, Leone and Drifter, Skye and Onyx at Nine Standards Rigg

🐾 🐾

A NEW CHAPTER FOR APRICOT

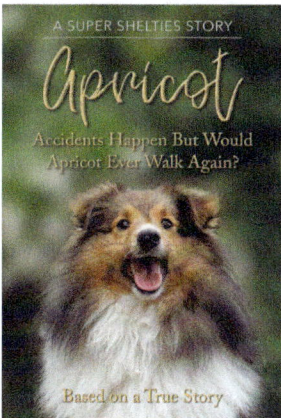

Apricot was only eleven weeks old when she broke her leg in two places. Luckily through lots of dedicated care Apricot fought herself back to fitness and the short story was released as an ebook this year. She is now living in the countryside and shared this update with us.

Inhale… Exhale… ahhhh the countryside. Fresh air, cows and wildlife! Baby Apricot moved from Copenhagen to a small village in the northern part of Denmark, Mariager which is located far away from the big city life. Moving was such a positive experience for our entire family.

Our family is enjoying our new house, especially the garden. We are blessed with 25 acres of land, where we can take daily trips. We are also gardening a lot. We planted a lot of roses in different colours, but mostly in an apricot-peachy colour. We also planted some vegetables which our dogs enjoy stealing directly from the dirt. All the activity is helping Apricot with her paw and making it stronger. Even the long hikes are not bothering her anymore.

On May 17th Apriocotta became a big sister to a border collie brother Bumblebee. He is so annoying, he bites her behind the ears and steals all the toys, but at the end of the day, she loves him very much. The future will surely bring some more life to our modern farm. We are hoping for chickens, sheep and maybe rabbits.

SENIOR SHELTIES

Shelties are majestic at any age but they certainly don't stay with us long enough. Let's celebrate these gorgeous senior shelties that are still living life to the full, extra white furs and all!

Roxy

Roxy is 12.5 years old living in Norfolk, UK.

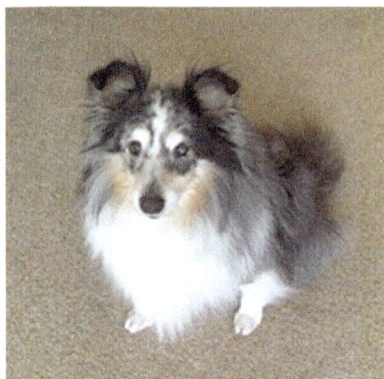

Pepper

Aged 12 and a half from Milnrow, Rochdale, UK.

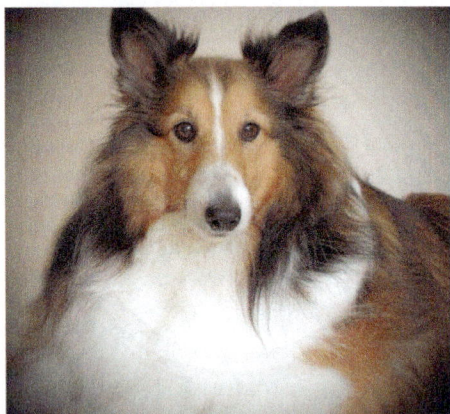

Teddy

Teddy is 11 and a half from Apple Valley, Minnesota, USA

Ted

Ted is 11 and a half years old from the UK

Sasha

Sasha is our first sheltie and a "golden oldie" at 11 (we still think she is gorgeous) from New Forest, Ringwood, UK.

SHELTIES IN DISGUISE

Shelties love being part of all the activities and there's nothing a sheltie won't do for a yummy treat – match made in heaven! Take a peek of some of these super smart shelties getting involved in the festivities!

Bentley says 'Yee Haw! I'm a Cowboy!' Make sure you watch out for Sheriff Leone though!

Is it a sheltie or the Loch Ness monster?

Aline getting into the Easter spirit

Amigo was ready to support his football team at the 2020 Eurocup, Go Denmark!

Toby, waiting with his kitty pal for trick or treaters

Leone from Ottawa is a real superstar, look at how dashing he is in his outfits!

IN HONOUR OF GRACIE MAY

Story by Russ Akehurst

My aunt Grace Aldridge was affectionately known as Gracie May. She was from Brighton and bred shelties in the '70s, '80s and '90s. My parents wouldn't allow me to have a dog and so it was lovely to be able to spend time with my aunt and go for long walks with her and her shelties. I can never remember her having less than four at a time.

Unfortunately, she tragically died on Sunday 31st May 1998. She had previously moved from Brighton to a village near Littlehampton called Lyminster and walked her dogs daily across the fields from her home to the nearby town of Arundel. Sadly on that Sunday, something happened and along with two of her four shelties, they were trampled to death by a herd of cows. Thankfully two of her dogs survived.

Since then I have always loved the breed and longed for one of my own.

I was really lucky to find my own Gracie May. For the past 13 years, I was the dog warden for Adur and Worthing Councils in West Sussex. I mentioned to everyone

I met that if they heard of a sheltie that needed rehoming to please bear me in mind.

My partner had worked at the Shoreham Dogs Trust rehoming centre for 27 years so with both of us working in rescue, we couldn't have bought a puppy. I knew that one day I would be in the right place at the right time.

How right I was, one Tuesday last December, I had just returned from a holiday abroad and was back at work when my mobile rang. The lady explained that she was a sheltie breeder and had heard on the grapevine that I was looking for an adult sheltie – was I interested?

Without hesitation, I replied yes and it was arranged to see the dog on Sunday. I'm not sure if I even asked the sex or colour because it certainly didn't matter to me as long as it was a sheltie.

Come the Sunday my partner, myself and the three dogs we had at the time went to the breeders home and met Millie (now called Gracie May). The breeder explained that she is MDR1+ and also carries one copy of the Collie Eye Anomaly mutation so being a responsible breeder she wouldn't use her for breeding.

It didn't matter to us, we wanted her. We brought her home last December and renamed her Gracie May in honour of my aunt. She is now three, living her best life happily with us in Norfolk, UK

❀ ❀ ❀ ❀ ❀ ❀ ❀ ❀ ❀ ❀ ❀ ❀ ❀ ❀ ❀ ❀
❀ ❀ ❀ ❀ ❀ ❀ ❀ ❀ ❀ ❀ ❀ ❀ ❀ ❀ ❀ ❀

The deadly stampede

Cows trample pensioner as she walks her dogs

A PENSIONER was trampled to death by a herd of cows as she walked her dogs on a public footpath.

Grace Aldridge was found alongside the corpses of two of her four shelties. One of the surviving animals was howling at her feet.

It is believed she was crushed under the hooves of more than 50 cows and a bull which were grazing in the field where she walked.

The Health and Safety Executive yesterday opened an official inquiry.

It is not known whether the dogs incited the cows to stampede. But experts said cattle could react aggressively if they felt they or their calves were threatened.

Mrs Aldridge, a widow of 67, was well-known in the village of Lyminster near Arun-

By THOMAS HARDING

del, West Sussex, for her love of dogs. She had lived alone since the death of her husband more than 30 years ago and had no children.

Neighbours say she had walked many times in the same field without mishap.

A couple out walking found her battered and bloodied body on Sunday evening at the side of a field which is owned by Broomhurst Farm.

The footpath she had been walking along runs from the back of Lyminster Church, where Mrs Aldridge was verger, to the farm. The Reverend John Sless, 62, said

the village was in shock. He added yesterday: 'She was dearly loved by everybody and will be very sadly missed. People would always see her walking her dogs irrespective of the weather. It is a terrible thing to have happened.'

The vicar's wife Marlene, 60, added: 'I sat with her in church yesterday morning. We don't exactly know what happened but I can't bear to think about it.'

Police said they would not be opening a criminal inquiry into the case.

Detective Inspector Dick Shelton, of Sussex police, said: 'Early indications are that this was a very tragic

accident. For some reason, the cows acted unpredictably.'

There have been six deaths caused by cattle attacks on humans since 1996 and the HSE says it has investigated 16 major incidents.

Spokesman Janet Connah said: 'We require that employers do not put other people, for instance members of the public, at risk by their work activities.

'This means we will investigate whether there was danger to people crossing this field with the cattle in it.'

The cattle involved were a Charolais-Limousin cross, bred for beef.

Victim: Mrs Aldridge with one of her beloved dogs

SHELTIE ARTISTS

We had some submissions from our talented readers of their incredible sheltie art to share with you. Aren't they amazing? They can even take commissions and have kindly provided contact details so you can get your own custom art piece of your pooch too!

Sophie Parkhill is a wildlife artist and pet portrait artist based in North Wales. Most recently, she painted these two very beautiful shelties Candy and Willow. Find Sophie at SP Wildlife Art www.spwildlifeart.com or on Facebook / Instagram: spwildlifeart

Pet Portraits by Louise undertakes commissions, for more information email: torriglen6@gmail.com

Sarah-Jane began a side business of illustrations during lockdown. Find Sarah-Jane at www.instagram.com/Pucci_illustrations with links to her Etsy and RedBubble on there too.

instagram @skylafraydesigns
website www.skylafraydesigns.com
email skylafraydesigns@gmail.com

Skyla Fray Designs

graphic design and fine art.

HI THERE!

I'm Skyla, an Australian artist, graphic designer, and, above all, a Sheltie lover!

I have been making art my whole life, drawing inspiration from the things I love most. I decided to start my own business, doing what I love, in Year 12 (2020). It was last year, when I created a very special Sheltie design that captured the heart of many dog lovers. What began as one design grew into my 'Dog Love' Series representing over 110 breeds and is now growing into my dream. Little did I know, a Sheltie and an iPad were going to change my life.

CONTACT US!

We are committed to creating the design, logo, or product of your dreams! We have so much

Artwork by Charlotte at Lotti Brown Designs at www.lottibrowndesigns.com

WHAT MAKES A SHELTIE SO SPECIAL?

We asked our readers what makes shelties so special to them...

Shelties are the best antidepressants in the world. It doesn't matter how dark your days are because seeing those quizzical animated faces greeting us as we come home from work, you can't fail to smile.

I went through a very dark time last year as I lost Archie just before the country locked down [due to COVID-19]. His best mate Rolo was bereft for several months but then we got Bernie. He is cheeky, funny, loves our springer Freya and has put a big smile on all our faces.

Not only have I, like everyone had to deal with COVID, but also two ailing parents; one has Alzheimer's and the other is going blind. I had to give up my job in the NHS after 34 years last year to help my parents and I was in a very dark place.

My dogs have been my therapists and continue to be as my father is now in a nursing home but mum needs constant help from me and my sister. Bernie, Rolo and Freya are more than dogs they are my family, and they have given me the incentive to carry on with a very different life than what I had two years ago. Thanks to my stubborn, funny, loving, sensitive and very barky boy Archie, shelties will have my heart forever.

Julie Knee from Torquay, UK

My sheltie's name is Teddy and he is now 11.5 years of age. In November 2021 he had TPLO surgery which meant he had a steel replacement inserted into his right leg replacing his ACL tendon.

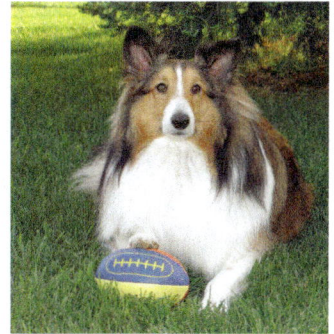

He has recovered very well but is now suffering from severe arthritis in his left ankle resulting in his left paw turning inward and a significant limp. He never complains and continues to smile and ask for butt scratches.

Very frequently he will lay and stare at me and when our eyes meet, I feel like our souls are exchanging hearts. He knows exactly what I'm saying and how I'm feeling. He is definitely an extension of me.

Julie Syverson from Apple Valley, Minnesota

Our puppy is Indiana 'Indy' Bones. We named him that because he found things we thought we lost forever and he's our little explorer.

We love the breed because they bring us so much joy. They are the sweetest, most inquisitive dogs I've ever been around and if I'm ever upset I just look at their little 'smiles' and it's like everything goes away.

Jennifer Vicente

WHAT MAKES A SHELTIE SO SPECIAL?

" For several years I owned long-haired miniature dachshunds. Then one day I met a lady walking a sheltie. This was my first encounter with the breed, and I was intrigued by this bright-eyed, inquisitive yet reserved dog. I jumped at the chance to have a sheltie when the opportunity arose.

Jordie was my first sheltie and as a puppy learned quickly to terrorise my dachshund with his never-ending play. Often, I would see a befuddled dachshund trudging past with a sheltie pulling on his tail.

Puppy training and socialisation were attempted with little success initially, the trainer left me with the advice that I simply had a high arousal dog and wished me luck. However, I was won over by this intensely loyal, intelligent, affectionate soul. His desire to please, his ability to understand emotion when a cuddle is needed and his complete trust and devotion.

For some time, I tried to find a companion for Jordie following the death of my last dachshund. Eventually, I was offered a sheltie from a breeder who felt he was not up to show standard. Bryn entered my life. Here is a different dog again, outgoing, eager to investigate, befriend any stranger and with an overwhelming desire to play from morning to night. With an endearing high-speed spinning dance of impatience whenever dinner time approaches, intensifying if there is a delay before the plate hits the floor.

The last piece of the puzzle is Charli. From the same breeder as Bryn and with the same father, she again was offered to me as being unlikely to succeed in the show ring. More reserved and anxious than her half-brother, she makes up for this in her tenacity and her independence. She is quite happy to wander around the garden on her own, making any sofa or high vantage point her own but she also is immensely affectionate and vocal in expressing her opinion.

At present then our family is complete. The three all have unique, individual personalities but what unites them is their loyalty, their energy, their love and their devotion to our family. To me, that's what makes shelties special. There is no other dog like them.

David Miller from New Zealand

Shelties must be one of the loyalist breeds. I have an 8 year old tricolour called Laddie. I can tell him off for wanting to chase anything on two wheels but soon realise I can't stay mad at him when he always seems to be smiling at me.

I have met so many local friends just by walking a sheltie regularly. Most of all he makes me smile and after the uncertain times we live in that is priceless.

Gary Walker of Hull in East Yorkshire UK

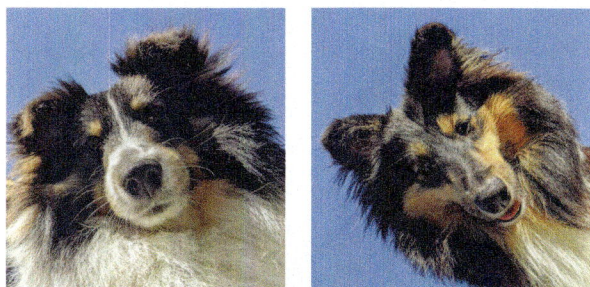

These photos (left) of Lincoln, Nessie and Bentley make me so happy in these trying times. It helps to not take life too seriously and remember the simple things in life, like blue skies, a beautiful day and beautiful shelties can make all problems fade away into the distance.

Allison Begnell

Shelties bring a never-ending love. From the moment 25 years ago when I set eyes on our first sheltie, Lassie, it was love at first sight. She was so loyal. My second girl Carly was my heart girl, the love of my life. She was such a beautiful, pure, elegant little lady and the love I still have for her is overwhelming.

Talia has shown me how to love again after losing Carly and is the most affectionate sheltie I've owned. She loves to sit and snuggle and when I look into her twinkling eyes she just melts my heart. It's an overwhelming love I feel for her... whoever said diamonds are a girls best friend never had a sheltie as most of my treasured thoughts are with Lassie, my heart girl Carly. And now my happiest moments are spent with Talia and my grandpups Teddy and Mia.

Jeanette Fellas from Norfolk, UK

River at agility

L to R: Cody, Prince, Milo, Luca and Shandy (inset)

A HISTORY OF OAKCROFT

It was through my sister that my love of shelties began as she had a sable and white sheltie called Misty who I adored. My sister used to breed and show rough collies which introduced me to handling at a very young age. I showed a couple of her bitches at some collie shows and qualified at the *London and Provincial Collie Club Championship Show* in 1965 for *Crufts* 1966.

I had to wait a long time to get my own sheltie. It wasn't until I got married and we moved into our first house that I was able to have one of my own in 1982. In the meantime, I collected sheltie memorabilia, ornaments and read all the books I came across on shelties. I started training with my first sheltie Shandy, as I wanted a nice well-behaved dog to take out. Shortly after I went to an exemption show and was placed so that this encouraged me to start off doing competitive obedience as a hobby. I had several shelties that won through the early classes to compete in the more advanced A and B classes.

Although I had been a regular visitor to *Crufts* to see the obedience competitions, I liked to watch the breed judging. It wasn't until 2000 when I was offered the opportunity to have my first show dog Milo, *Kamarlee Laiderettes Milo JW* that I began my journey in breed judging and showing. I started showing him in 2001; he won the minor puppy class at his first championship show at *Birmingham National* and that was when I truly got the bug and converted to the show scene.

In 2003 a friend used Milo as a sire and had four bitches and I was persuaded to have a daughter from him. I bred from her and subsequently had the joy of having my very first litter in 2005 which started my *Oakcroft* line.

In 2010 I had a *Rannerdale* bitch from Ann Stafford. Although she didn't end up in the show ring she was very influential in my breeding, producing two champions *Ch Oakcroft Star Force JW*, Cody, who got his title in 2016 and then his half-brother *Ch Oakcroft Prince Charming JW*, Prince, in 2017.

I was also lucky to have one of Cody's daughters *Carolelen Classic Star By Oakcroft*

JW, Pixie, who has also won a CC and Reserve CC but like others, due to Covid, there has not been too many shows. Instead, I have used the opportunity to have some puppies from her and my old gentleman *Oakcroft Cosmic Encounter,* Cosmo, and so have kept two promising bitches which I am hoping to show later this year.

In 2018 Tatjana and Milan from the Czech Republic contacted me to use *Oakcroft Goldsmith,* Monty and after many messages, Milan came over to mate his bitch Breeze. When I saw photos of the puppies I was so impressed I asked if there was the possibility to have one. Then in early November, I went over to see them and I decided to not only have a boy from the litter but a bitch as well so Luca and Alisa came over the week before Christmas.

I have successfully been able to show Luca and he gained his JW just before the Covid lockdown. He has recently gone back to Milan to show at the *World Dog Show*; he won his open class CAC and Res CACIB and Res Best Dog and at the speciality show the next day he won the open class CAC. In the intervening years, I was also encouraged to start judging. It was in 2008 that I had my first judging appointment and to further my knowledge of the breed have attended several breed seminars and assessments.

I have judged at various shows around the UK and also had an opportunity to go to Norway to judge there which was certainly a wonderful experience.

I had also completed the Kennel Club requirements to judge at championship shows and although I was unable to do my first CC judging appointment for Bournemouth Canine Association in 2020 [due to Covid] I was luckily able to do it in August this year instead.

By Val Winfield

Tina now (above) and when she was rescued (inset)

THE RIGHT TIME FOR A RESCUE

After a drastic change to my personal circumstances, I was no longer in a position to breed another litter and consequently my line came to an end. I continued to enjoy competing in various activities with my remaining shelties until inevitably there was only one. This little girl had never been on her own. We were both sorely missing her brother but she was taking it particularly badly, she needed a companion.

Soon after I heard about a possible rescue, this sounded very promising. My little girl needed a new companion, we had the space and this little girl needed a home. I made enquiries and was successful in securing her. She had a long journey to get here, she arrived grossly over weight, not house-trained and scared of everything. It was obvious she had not had much of a life.

Gradually and with careful nurturing she was introduced to so many new experiences. Now nearly two years later, with the help of my own little girl as her mentor, she is leading the kind of life she should always have had. With her breeding days behind her she is enjoying life, at training classes, is working towards her Silver Good Citizen award, attends Rally and has just started some agility.

SHOW WINS

We'd like to send massive congratulations to readers who wrote in with some fantastic placements in shows over the past year. Congratulations to these gorgeous examples of our wonderful breed and their owners and breeders!

Milly, Australian Champion *Peerielee Colours Of The Wind* was awarded Best Neuter, Best Blue and Best coated Bitch in Shetland Sheepdog Club of Queensland Australia open show, along with Reserve Challenge Neuter Bitch in the championship show all at 8 and a half years old! Photographed by Patrik Berger.

Bentley, *Sharndah Burn For U*, awarded Best Tri/Bi Black in the Shetland Sheepdog Club of Queensland Australia open show along with Best Minor Dog in both the open and championship shows. Photographed by Patrik Berger.

SUCCESS AT THE WORLD DOG SHOW 2021

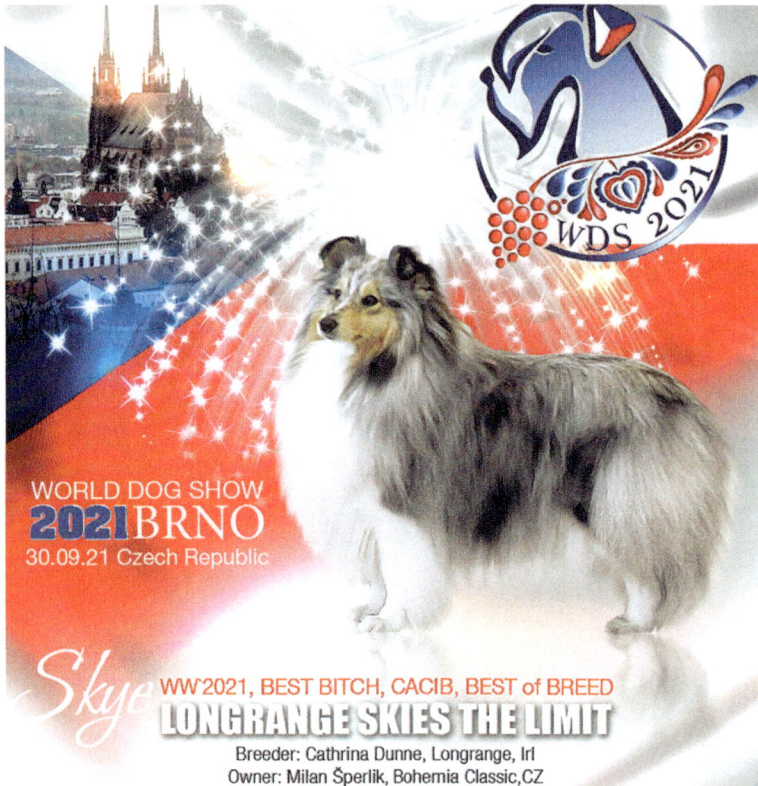

WORLD DOG SHOW
2021 BRNO
30.09.21 Czech Republic

Skye WW'2021, BEST BITCH, CACIB, BEST of BREED
LONGRANGE SKIES THE LIMIT
Breeder: Cathrina Dunne, Longrange, Irl
Owner: Milan Šperlik, Bohemia Classic, CZ

The Bohemia Classic team have had many incredible placements in the past year with Skye winning Best Bitch and Best of Breed at the World Dog Show and wins for BISS Puppy and Junior classes and many more. Congratulations!

STAY CONNECTED!

We hope you've enjoyed the annual and look forward to sharing more stories and photos from the sheltie community next year. Thank you to everyone that sent in photos and stories – we couldn't make this book without you. If you'd like to keep up to date with our new projects and find out when submissions open for the *I Love Shelties Annual 2023*, sign up to our newsletter:

www.iloveshelties.com/newsletter

In the meantime, let us know what you thought of the book by leaving a review on Amazon and send us your photos of your pups enjoying their copy, we love to see your photos!

We'd love to invite you to our brand new *I Love Shelties* community on *Mighty Networks* to connect with other sheltie lovers around the world.

To join please visit **www.iloveshelties.com/connect** to find out more.

Follow I Love Shelties: www.facebook.com/ilovesheltiesworldwide

Email us at: hello@iloveshelties.com

NO OTHER BREED WILL DO

The sheltie is the breed for me, no other breed will do.

It has to be a sheltie, whether sable, tri or blue.

I got to own a sheltie when I was ten years old,

I had to train and care for her, by my parents I was told.

I've always had a sheltie, I couldn't be without,

I will always have a sheltie, of that, there is no doubt.

Some people say they're noisy, and what about the hair!

These are not my kind of people, and neither do I care.

Now so many years have passed with shelties by my side,

My heart is like a treasure trove, with the memories locked inside.

I love my loyal shelties, so beautiful and true,

The sheltie is the breed for me, no other breed will do.

Louise Saunders

Happy Boy Cracker, photo by Louise Saunders

Printed in Great Britain
by Amazon